FEISTY
and
FIERY
and
FIERCE

BADASS WOMEN TO LIVE YOUR LIFE BY FROM THE CELTIC NATIONS OF SCOTLAND, IRELAND AND WALES

MAIRI KIDD

BLACK & WHITE PUBLISHING

First published 2020
by Black & White Publishing Ltd
Nautical House, 104 Commercial Street
Edinburgh, EH6 6NF

1 3 5 7 9 10 8 6 4 2   20 21 22 23

ISBN: 978 1 78530 308 1

A CIP catalogue record for this book is available from the British Library.

Layout by Black & White
Printed and bound in Turkey by Imago

CONTENTS

IRELAND

WALES

To Carol Veronica Ashworth

a good woman (no matter what anyone says)

INTRODUCTION

THE WOMEN ARE MISSING

The saying goes that you cannot be what you cannot see. As with many 'truths universally acknowledged', it's true to a degree – and thankfully only to a degree. Since the mid-years of the nineteenth century, women have been breaking through all sorts of barriers to become university students, lawyers, doctors, politicians, sportspeople, police officers and more. These women could not see other women in further education, in the law, in the medical profession – they had to imagine themselves there. Among the significant obstacles they faced was the idea that women couldn't do things simply because they hadn't done those things before. From that position, it's a small step to conclude that women have never really done anything at all.

In our earliest representations of human figures, images of women proliferate. In prehistory, it seems, women had some power, and, generally speaking, we believe that peaceable societal groups proliferated in which measures of success were linked to community survival and wellbeing. But as prehistory gave way to history, societal shifts saw increasing militarisation. Male strength became key to success, which was reckoned in terms of conquest and expansion. Violent male gods suddenly rocked up in many societies across the world, and those gods weren't going to share the stage with anyone. The goddesses were written out, and women's power receded with them.

History is a narrative – our account of what happened in the past. One way of looking at it is that it is both the *story* and the *exercise* of power. And, because power has resided with men in most societies for around 3,500 years, history has tended to be written by men, for men, and about men. It has promoted entirely the idea that the stuff worth writing about is the stuff done by men.

There are two enormous and interrelated problems with this idea.

Firstly, it's marvellously short-sighted to believe that the only story worth the telling is that of power and privilege, conquest and war. This approach not only underserves the female half of humanity, it also underserves all 'ordinary' people, and of course it hugely underserves the 'conquered'. It is an exercise of power by a small group – and a cynical observer might note that this small group has been very successful to date in bringing the world to its knees. (In this context, it's interesting to note how often climate change denial goes hand in hand with misogyny and white supremacy. Progress in terms of equalities and carbon emissions ultimately threatens the interest of those doing very well out of exploiting the world and its people.)

Secondly, there are obvious omissions from the narrative, even in its own terms. Women, Indigenous people and others have always overstepped the boundaries of lives circumscribed by others, to achieve remarkable things. But the narrative plays a purpose – it perpetrates inequality. To ensure it stands up, those stories that would undermine it must be excised. This happens both in terms of the records we keep and in what we allow to happen in the first place. Hatshepsut the (female) Pharoah's name is literally chipped off the pyramids. Peaceful medieval Scottish monarch Gruach is reinvented as Shakespeare's scheming harridan Lady Macbeth. Inconvenient women across Europe are denounced as witches, and many die for it.

CAREFUL AT THE INTERSECTION

Intersectionality is the idea that a person or group possessing more than one characteristic that may result in their being discriminated against may face unique challenges due to the overlap between different types of discrimination. The concept was coined in the United States by legal scholar and civil rights activist Kimberlé Crenshaw, and is still perhaps best illustrated by her example of Black women and the automobile industry. The industry has Black workers and it has women workers. But its Black workers are men on the machine floor, and its women are white office workers. The Black woman fits in neither place; she is on the intersection. There is no support for her unless we understand intersectionality.

Sex is a key factor in discrimination. It intersects with class, ethnicity, nationality, language and other considerations to further achieve the erasure of women's experiences from history.

THE BIG AND THE SMALL

This book looks at women from three countries: Ireland (the North and the Republic), Scotland and Wales. These are the smaller countries within our island group, and the tangram they form on the map has a large and obvious gap at the centre in the shape of England. Ireland, Scotland and Wales have been shaped by England, and have shaped England in turn. At some point in their history, all three have been at war with England, in truce with England and in union with England. Their direct relationships with one another have varied. Ireland and Scotland have perhaps the closest link; Irish settlers to Scottish territory gave the country its name and much of its early history, and cultural and political exchange has significantly influenced the story of the two countries ever since. Ireland and Wales form two ends of a frequently used sea route, and since early times their populations have crossed both ways. Wales is geographically more distant from Scotland, but in its Welsh language preserves some of the history of early Scotland, where tribal groups and confederations spoke languages from the same branch of the Celtic tree.

Since history is written by men for men, and by victors for victors, the history of the British Isles has tended to favour the story of the males of England. The end result is that most citizens of Ireland, Scotland and Wales know each other's histories less well than they know the history of their larger neighbour in the middle. This book aims to right that wrong in a small way, with a short *her*story of each country to place individual women's stories in context.

STARTING THE SEARCH

Scottish poet Violet Jacob once wrote a poem of longing for a dead love. It talks of a space in the shadows between the dark and the light, where a ghost might reach out and take the hand of one still living. The poem frames the thought as that of a man, but of course it is in truth a woman's poem, and offers us a good place to begin to think about where we might find the women in our three countries' pasts.

Occasionally we find the women are already there in the light. Gráinne Ní Mháille/Grace O'Malley (see page 103) is an Irish example of a woman whose place in history is significant, and who is remembered – and sometimes misremembered – as a result.

More often, we find women in the shadows. We may have to dig to find their stories, considering traditional or literary sources to supplement official accounts, and reading between the lines. Some documents we need to read *past* – women regularly appear in recorded history in relation to male stories, and in this manner they are often poorly served.

If the record does badly by women overall, it does especially badly by the 'ordinary' women of any given place. Violet Jacob adopted in her poetry the voices of the working folk of the North-East of Scotland – the ploughmen and farm-wives, fisherfolk and servant quines. She was not, herself, of this class, but rather was born to a Scottish laird and a Welsh landowner's daughter. The chances are higher of us knowing the stories of women of similar privilege, and lower for the working classes. Why otherwise should wealthy, privileged and well-connected Englishwoman Florence Nightingale be lauded for her Crimean service while her working-class equivalent Betsi Cadwaladr (see page 177) was all but forgotten for 150 years? Or an online outcry occur in April 2020 when Scotland's Health Secretary Jeanne Freeman announced that Glasgow's temporary coronavirus treatment facility would be named not after Florence Nightingale, but after Maryhill-born Sister Louisa Jordan, heroine of the First World War?

The further back we go, the more the 'ordinary' women disappear, as records become scanter and the pool of people keeping those records becomes smaller, more male and more privileged. It is true, however, that records of women exist even in earlier periods, but still they go uncelebrated. So we find that Scotland's Agnes Campbell (see page 45), the most successful Edinburgh printer of the seventeenth century, has been neglected and instead the impression is given that commerce in that era was an arena of male-only success. Esther Inglis, illuminator and miniaturist (see page 31), is forgotten, while we remember that Nicholas Hilliard painted Mary, Queen of Scots. It is impossible to imagine the Scottish Gaelic literature of the seventeenth and eighteenth centuries without its women poets, a book's editor tells me on stage at a book festival. Yet his anthology has a ratio of 4:1 of male-authored work to female, and neglects to mention that some of Scottish Gaeldom's iconic female voices suffered active suppression in their lifetimes on the basis of their sex.

That last anecdote, of course, underlines the fact that our countries' stories are still told by men more often than by women. When the Scottish campaign group ROAR published its 2018 count of Scottish literature opportunities, it found that women are published less than men, review less and are reviewed less, and are even programmed less at book festivals. In response, the narrative of the meritocracy is trotted out again and again – women simply aren't as good as men. 'Just try harder, dear,' as one comment on the ROAR research put it.

The truth, of course, is that women *did* and *do* have to work harder. Agnes Campbell's example illustrates this point amply; she became successful despite a significant disadvantage: the law forbade her entering contracts in her own right on the basis she was a married woman. All her competitors had to do was issue their books; Agnes had to pursue an Act of Parliament at the same time, just for the permission to run her business. 'Try harder, dear,' indeed.

Violet Jacob's poem also reminds us that we can overlook what is right in front of our noses. In writing of love between two men, she may have given voice to the feelings of her only son, Harry, who died at the Somme and was quite probably gay. On paper, she's an unlikely straight ally to LGBTQI+ people, but that may have been what she was. We can easily fall into a rather smug trap of believing our predecessors were more 'primitive' than we are with our 'modern' attitudes. And then we find Ireland's Peg Plunkett (see page 127) writing an erotic memoir, or Nell Gwynn scoring points off Charles II (see page 169) like an early Phoebe Waller-Bridge.

MAKING A START

This book does not aim to give a complete account of the women of Scotland, Ireland, and Wales; such a task would be impossible. Instead it selects a 'coven' of thirteen women per country whose stories challenge the idea that women have never done anything worth recording. Hopefully these stories will entertain you, enrage you, uplift you and inspire you to fight for an equal space for everyone in our countries' stories going forward.

SCOTLAND

WISEWOMEN AND WITCHES AND DAMN REBEL BITCHES

PRE~HERSTORY

Male-default thinking dominates much writing about prehistory, in which terms such as 'Mesolithic man' are prevalent. Fans of this style will no doubt argue that these terms are intended to indicate all humankind, but there is evidence that the effect is to erase women from the account. Prehistoric *woman*, of course, played her part in the world.

In Scotland, the first signs of human habitation date from around 12,000 BC; this is later than much of the rest of Europe due to adverse (COLD!) climactic conditions. By the Mesolithic era (10,000–5,000 BC), nomadic hunter-gatherers were setting up camp across the country. In the Neolithic era (4,000–2,000 BC), farming was introduced, with swathes of land cleared for crops and domestic animals. Neolithic societies built great stone circles, large communal tombs and other monuments, many of which survive today, together with a number of their settlements and dwellings.

The Bronze Age was quite late to reach Scotland as metalworking knowledge spread slowly from the south. Larger settlements developed and many cultural changes took place, such as individual burial practices in place of communal tombs. By the Iron Age, Celtic culture was established in Scotland. In the first century AD, the invading Romans called the various tribal groupings 'Caledonii' and eventually withdrew from 'Caledonia' in the face of ferocious guerilla warfare.

Women's status in prehistoric Scotland cannot be assumed to have been low. In 2009 a dig at a Neolithic site in Orkney yielded a small carved stone figure, apparently human, and tentatively identified as female. Prior to that discovery, the earliest sculpture of a human form ever found in Scotland was at Ballachulish in the West Highlands; it dates from around 600 BC and is also a representation of a woman. Some sources tell us Celtic women took an active part in warfare and politics in other parts of Britain. If they did, they may also have done so in Scotland.

EARLY HERSTORY

The 'Scotti' who give Scotland its modern name in fact originated in Ireland. These Gaelic-speaking peoples began to settle south-west Scotland from around AD 200, establishing the kingdom of Dál Riáta by the fifth century AD. The kingdom was regularly engaged in conflict with the people of Ulster over the North Channel of the Irish Sea, with the Britons in Strathclyde, and with the Picts in the north and east. The emerging kingdom of Northumbria and Viking raids from the sea added to Dál Riáta's troubles, and by the late seventh century AD its power was on the wane. By that point, however, Gaelic culture had a foothold across the country, aided by the spread of Celtic Christianity from the monastery founded by the Irish missionary Columba at Iona in the sixth century AD.

Women rather disappear in discussion of the Gaelic expansion into Scotland although, of course, they made the self-same treacherous sea-crossing as the Dál Riátan menfolk. Christianity, in its core concept of a single male deity, displaced what were probably more equal-opportunities beliefs in earlier Scotland and Ireland. Some women professed a profound Christian faith of their own and established nunneries across the country. In AD 697 women's rights were enshrined in law by abbot Adamnán of Iona, whose 'Law of the Innocents' sought to protect the rights of women, children and the clergy. The law supposedly was inspired by a dream of Adamnán's in which Ireland appeared to him personified as a woman. It specified harsh punishment for anyone guilty of an attack on a woman, including rape and offences against the chastity of noblewomen, and for anyone permitting such an attack to take place. Women were not to be forced to take part in combat and ideally nothing should interfere with their right to die unmolested in their own beds. Should a woman commit murder, arson or desecration of a place of worship, she should not be killed but set adrift in a boat with a paddle and a pail of gruel; in this manner only God could kill her.

Of the lives of Pictish and Celtic Briton women in Scotland, we know little beyond occasional glimpses in the shadows. In AD 843, tradition has it that King Kenneth MacAlpin united the Picts and Scots to form the Kingdom of Alba – Scotland's Gaelic name into the present day. His achievement is said to have been in part due to a Pictish mother; Pictish succession was perhaps matrilineal.

THE KINGDOM OF SCOTS

Kenneth MacAlpin's descendants styled themselves Rí Alban (King of Alba) for their control of a territory that was rather fluid, beginning north of the River Forth and reaching as far north as Moray and west to Strathclyde. Over the next hundred years, Strathclyde too became part of 'Scotia'. King David I established the royal burghs, a system of coinage and a series of legal and land reforms. The English border remained unstable until the Treaty of York settled it in much the same location as in the present day in 1237. In 1266, the Treaty of Perth returned the Western Isles and west coast from Norse to Scottish control – although the Lords of the Isles were effectively autonomous from the Scottish crown.

In the 1300s, the Wars of Independence sought to end control of England in Scottish affairs; Robert Bruce and his successors eventually achieved this aim, with the support of France. This 'Auld Alliance' saw strong Scottish–French links develop, particularly in the era of the Stuarts.

Women are by no means absent from accounts of these times. The Bruce women and other female Bruce supporters were significant, and suffered greatly as political pawns during the Wars of Independence. In the west, Devorgilla of Galloway and Amy of Garmoran were key Gaelic power players, but in both cases their interests were significantly affected by male power-plays.

STUART SCOTLAND

The Stuarts (originally Stewart) came to the throne through a marriage between Marjorie, daughter of Robert Bruce, and Robert, High Steward of Scotland; their son Robert became King Robert II in 1371. The Stuarts faced ongoing challenge from England, from their own nobles and from Gaelic power in the west, but from the reign of James I onwards they gradually consolidated power in the monarchy. Well-chosen marriages promoted diplomatic links, annexed territory, and gave Scotland a series of impressive Queens Consort from England's Joan Beaufort, who escaped the assassins who killed her husband James I, to Denmark's Margaret, who brought Orkney and Shetland as her dowry in 1468. These women often served as regents – being a Stuart king was not an occupation conducive to making old bones and their children tended to inherit the throne before they came of age.

The Highlands suffered under the Stuarts, who sought to suppress Gaelic power by eradicating the language, its culture and its aristocratic classes, but the south prospered as the Stuarts passed popular legislation, founded seats of learning and promoted the arts. James IV moved the court to Edinburgh before he died at the Battle of Flodden; through his marriage to Margaret Tudor, daughter of Henry VII of England, his great-grandson James VI would eventually become James I of England.

The Stuarts also gave Scotland that rare thing – a queen who ruled in her own right. Mary Stuart was just days old when her father, James V, died. She was raised at the French court and became Queen Consort of France by marriage to Francis II. When Francis died, she returned to Scotland. Mary was a Catholic queen in a country in the fervent grip of a Protestant Reformation. She managed to balance on this tightrope for a brief time but her rule was undermined by two unwise marriages, and eventually she was forced to abdicate in favour of her son James VI. She fled to England in hope of support from her cousin Elizabeth I – and instead got a long captivity, followed by the chop. On Elizabeth's death in 1603, Mary's son united the crowns of Scotland and England. Political union followed in 1707 – and is still a hot topic three centuries later.

The Stuarts also began Scotland's infamous record as one of the worst places in Europe for persecution of witches. There is a school of thought that the word 'witch' may be replaced in most instances in which it appears with 'woman', and it is true that the vast majority of those implicated in Scotland's witch panics were women. As far as we know, more than 3,800 'witches' lost their lives by a range of hideous means from burning to drowning, and many more were accused and suffered the horrors of interrogation and prosecution. The originator of this nightmare was none other than James VI, who took the particularly obtuse view that storms he and his new wife experienced during a sea journey had to be the work of some supernatural evil. As opposed to, you know, just the standard sort of weather most people expect on a Scottish ferry crossing.

ENLIGHTENMENT

The eighteenth and nineteenth centuries were mixed times for Scotland. No longer in a position to persecute witches or indeed anyone else, the Stuart monarchs had lost the throne and instead spent their time scheming from exile in France and Rome. Significant Scottish support for the Stuarts resulted in multiple armed uprisings; when the 'Jacobite' cause ultimately failed in 1746 at the Battle of Culloden, violent reprisals saw the Gaelic culture of the Highlands very seriously undermined. Women suffered significantly during this time, and many of their voices survive in both anonymous and attested song and poetry. The Highlands and Islands subsequently suffered mass depopulation as absentee landlords bought up traditional clan lands and displaced people in favour of sheep farms. As the Clearances reached their height, Highlanders were funnelled into the British Army, where one Major General Wolfe infamously commented 'no great mischief if they fall'. Eventually the Land Wars saw the population gain crofting rights, and women took up pitchforks and poetry to contribute to this fight.

In the south, the significant scientific and cultural developments of the 'Scottish Enlightenment' saw Scotland placed firmly on the map as a world centre of culture. Through the eighteenth and nineteenth centuries, the country played its part in the development of many modern theories of philosophy, science, medicine and political economy. Women's contributions have often been downplayed, but of course they were there. And when Scottish technological advances helped pave the way for a new industrialised world, women, of course, contributed more than their fair share of labour to the effort.

THE MODERN ERA

At the dawn of the twentieth century, Scotland was highly industrialised with a particularly strong fishing industry. Herring girls gutted the catch and fishwives carried it to market and sold it. Some women even carried their menfolk onto their boats on their backs so the fishermen could put to sea in dry clothes.

Whether fisherfolk or farmers, Scottish communities faced disproportionately heavy losses in the First World War, and political unrest followed as both rural and urban areas saw economic stagnation. The women and men of 'Red Clydeside' gave birth to the modern-day labour movement – and drew tanks to George Square as the government sought to suppress any potential revolutionary uprising Glasgow might have in mind.

The Second World War saw some uplift in Scottish manufacturing fortunes, but in the postwar period, traditional industries went into sharp decline. Advances in women's rights stalled somewhat at this point, as advances towards equality tend to do when discontent of all sorts is rife. Scotland saw some economic relief upon the discovery of North Sea oil in the 1970s, but political disillusion continued, particularly when Margaret Thatcher's government introduced the deeply unpopular 'Poll Tax' to Scotland early.

A devolved Scottish Parliament opened in 1999 and has seen significant steps forward in terms of representation of and for women. Three Scottish parties have had female leaders; two of these women have been openly gay. One of these women, Ruth Davidson, became the first UK party leader to have a baby while in office. Another, Nicola Sturgeon, has served as First Minister and chose to gender-balance her cabinet to signal 'that the business of redressing the gender balance in public life starts right here in government'.

An independence referendum in 2014 returned a 'No' vote in the face of promises of the devolution of additional powers to Scotland. Scotland returned a decisive 'Remain' vote in the Brexit Referendum of 2016 and remains strongly pro-European. Who can say what Scotland's constitutional future is? Watch this space, and while you wait, read on for some inspiring, uplifting and occasionally enraging stories of Scottish womanhood through the ages.

"When people have lived for generations on one piece of land they have quite the memory."

JULIE GIBSON
ORKNEY ARCHAEOLOGIST

THE WOMAN AT SCAR

ELDER

I n 1985 a farmer named John Deerness was walking along the beach at Scar on the island of Sanday in Orkney when he discovered a number of human bones jutting out of a sandbank. A few days earlier the island had been battered by a ferocious storm, and the wind and waves had ripped back sand and soil from the coast to reveal the bones. John Deerness assumed he had stumbled over the grave of a sailor lost at sea. He picked up a small lead token, about a quarter of an inch in diameter, and took it home. He showed it to a neighbour, who thought it looked like part of a car battery. John Deerness placed it in a kitchen drawer where it remained until his death.

Six years later archaeologist Julie Gibson heard about the bones in the bank at Scar. At that point in her career, Julie hadn't excavated an Iron Age burial and decided to visit the site at Scar in the hope it might be older than John Deerness had first thought. She located the bones, and two lumps of rusted iron which might be boat rivets. She visited John Deerness's widow, who showed her the little lead object her husband had found. Finally the car battery identification was laid to rest – in fact, the object was a Viking lead weight, deposited on Sanday some 1,100 years before.

The race was now on to excavate the site before another winter storm could sweep it out to sea. A team of rescue archaeologists began to dig in November 1991, working with limited daylight and in challenging weather conditions. They succeeded in saving what remained of a Viking boat burial containing three skeletons and a rich range of grave goods. It was an unusual boat grave, as most burials of this type contain only one person. There were grains of sand in the caulking of the boat that indicated it had been built in Norway. It was not large, and probably had been transported to Orkney aboard a larger boat. Whether the people buried within it were born in Norway too is unknown.

The largest skeleton was that of a man who lay crouched in the stern of the boat. He was 5 foot 11 inches in height and probably in his thirties when he died. It was not possible to determine the sex of the child. It died at the age of ten or eleven, and lay on its back beside the woman. The woman lay straight on her back, in the centre of the boat. She was a considerable age, probably in her seventies, when she died.

We cannot and will never be able to say exactly who these people were, nor what linked them. We can be relatively sure that they were connected, because there seems no reason for three unrelated individuals to have been buried in such a way.

Were they family? The woman could not have been the child's mother. She might have been the man's mother, or his grandmother. He might have been the child's father. It seems unlikely that the woman was the man's wife, at least in any conventional sense we understand today.

It seems likely that they died around the same time, as a boat burial was not likely to have been opened on multiple occasions. Perhaps they succumbed to the same illness. Perhaps they died in an accident. Perhaps one or more of them was sacrificed to accompany the third to the afterlife.

Some have suggested that the man and child were sacrificed to accompany the woman, on the basis that her great age might have marked her out as a person of great standing. The man's skeleton was suggestive of hard physical labour, possibly rowing, and of fighting with a sword. If he was sacrificed to accompany the woman, perhaps he was her servant. His grave goods are rather rich to support this theory – a sword, arrows, a bone and antler comb and whalebone gaming pieces – but these might have been bestowed upon him after death.

The woman was buried with a range of items including brooches, spindle weights, an iron sickle and shears for cutting cloth or wool. The most spectacular item by far is her whalebone plaque, decorated with two carved horses or dragons. These plaques were used, some experts think, for smoothing linen, by rubbing the fabric against the smooth whalebone with a heated glass weight.

This interpretation is based on a wealthy woman's burial in Birka in Sweden in which a plaque and glass weight were found together. The Scar plaque had no glass smoother, and it does not show any significant signs of wear; this is true of many of these items recovered from other graves.

In absence of smoothers in many graves, recent scholarship has considered whether the gorgeous plaques had other meanings. Possibly they represent female labour, in contributing to the wealth and success of a home and community. Possibly they represent wealth, being made of a rare commodity. Possibly they have a deeper significance, even a religious one. One theory says that flax in Norse mythology was 'the seed of a woman', and related to fertility, and the smoothing of linen cloth on whalebone plaques was in some way related to worship of Freyja, goddess of fertility. The woman at Scar might, if this is true, even have been a priestess.

Whether the woman at Scar's plaque was a practical item used in the home or a symbolic one employed in worship, a treasured personal possession or one gifted to her in death for religious reasons, it is indicative of a level of power and wealth. Norse women of the Viking era by no means enjoyed equality with men, but they perhaps had somewhat better rights than their contemporaries in other European societies. They could own and inherit money and property, and they could trade – scales and other items associated with this activity are found in some women's graves. They could be patrons of art, seek punishment of anyone who harassed or raped them, and they could seek a divorce. They travelled with men to battle, on raiding parties and to new lands. As one example, the sagas tell us that Gudrid Thorbjarnardóttir travelled to Vinland – America – in the face of perils both natural and supernatural, and gave birth to her son Snorri there. Who knows what great journeys the woman at Scar made before she was laid with her companions and her riches in a Norwegian boat on a Scottish island, outfitted to voyage to the lands of the dead?

LIVE YOUR LIFE BY THE WOMAN AT SCAR

A recent Australian study of Viking-era Norse burials in England purposely ignored the grave goods found with each burial and instead focused on osteological signs indicative of gender. A number of burials identified as male owing to the presence of swords or other weapons in fact were reclassified as female. Archaeology, it seems, has a gender bias. Take inspiration from this fact and try to refrain from categorising preferences, attributes and so forth as 'male' or 'female'. This behaviour perpetrates inequalities, especially when applied to children.

On the subject of biases, remember the woman buried at Scar when you think or talk of older people. The great age the Scar woman had attained may have contributed to her status in society; it certainly did nothing to harm it. In many societies elderly people are venerated for their accumulated wisdom and their perspective. Their value is not counted in their ability to produce material goods; instead they embody continuity and have a role in guiding the young. Look to the ways in which elderly people in the UK were discussed during the early stages of the coronavirus outbreak and you will see that we do not always hold the elderly in such respect.

ISEABAL NÍ MHEIC CAILÉIN

POET

Three poems by Iseabal Ní Mheic Cailéin survive in the Book of the Dean of Lismore. The Book – a hand-written manuscript – is a sort of new writing magazine, 1500s-style. It preserves a range of texts in Scots, Gaelic, Irish and Latin and was compiled by a Perthshire churchman and his collaborators.

Two of the poems by Iseabal in the manuscript are in the tradition of 'courtly love'. These are 'Is mairg dá ngalar an grádh' (*Woe to the one whose sickness is love*) and 'Atá fleasgach ar mo thí' (*There is a young man in pursuit of me*). 'Courtly love' is a term coined to describe a literary style popular throughout Europe in the Middle Ages; essentially, a knight and married lady fall in love and swoon around desiring one another in the most passionate terms while being very chaste and godly and therefore not actually doing anything about it. Here's Iseabal palpitating in style:

Atá fleasgach ar mo thí
A Rí na ríogh go rí leis
a bheith sínte ré mo bhroinn
agus a chom ré mo chneis.

A young man is in pursuit of me
Oh King of Kings, may he succeed
Would that he were stretched alongside me
with his body pressed to my breast.

So far, so Mills & Boon. The third poem by Iseabal is rather different, being a boast about her household priest's penis and its prodigious size, rigidity and vigour. Ooh-er missus or, in Gaelic, *obh obh a Leagsaidh*.

Iseabal's identity has been subject to some debate. Literally the name means 'Isobel, daughter of the Son of Colin'. 'Son of Colin' is a kenning for the Earl of Argyll, and so Iseabal's name and rough dates imply that she was either the daughter of Colin Campbell, 1st Earl of Argyll (d. 1493) with his wife Isobel Stewart, or Colin and Isobel's granddaughter via their son Archibald and daughter-in-law Elizabeth Stewart. Some Gaelic scholars have suggested that Isobel Stewart, the 1st Earl's wife, was actually the author of the poems, and that the Gaelic for 'daughter' was written before her husband's name almost as one might write 'Mrs' in English.

The distinctly naughty tone of Iseabal's surviving poetry has flummoxed some modern thinkers, who struggle to imagine that either the wife *or* the daughter of an earl would sit around composing poetry in which a married lady fantasises about a gallant knight, let alone an ode to a penis. It is, of course, possible that the poetry was meant to be read lightly, that it was a nothing more than an exercise in composition, or perhaps it's just that Iseabal's time was bolder than our own and she was a serious badass.

LIVE YOUR LIFE BY ISEABAL

Frankness in discussing body parts and sex hasn't moved forward that much in the five hundred years that have passed since Iseabal's day. In early 2020, actress Emma Watson caused a stir when she announced that she was a member of a website focused on female sexual pleasure. Take a leaf out of Iseabal's book (and Emma's) and ditch the shame when it comes to bodies and pleasure.

"Éistibh a luchd an tighe-se
re scél na mbod bríoghmhar
do shanntaich mo chridhe-sa
cuid dana scéalaibh do
sgríobhadh."

"Listen, people of this house
to the story of the substantial penis
that made my heart greedy
I will write more of the tale."

ISEABAL NÍ MHEIC CAILÉIN
ÉISTIBH A LUCHD AN TIGHE-SE
C. 1500

"Item, for x 1/2 elne
Bertane cloth to be sarkis
to the Moris"

JAMES IV'S LORD HIGH TREASURER RECORDS
THE PURCHASE OF TEN AND A HALF ELLS OF BRETON CLOTH
FOR ELEN AND HER COMPANION'S SHIRTS OR SHIFTS
1506

ELEN MORE
WAITING WOMAN

We know nothing of Elen More's birth, of her childhood, her family and personal relationships – beyond the fact that she had a sister or close companion called Margaret – or of her interior life. She appears in records relating purely to her position as a waiting woman in the retinue of Lady Margaret, the daughter of James IV with his mistress Margaret Drummond. Later Elen joined the household of James's wife Margaret Tudor, a redoubtable woman who served as Regent for her son James V after his father was killed in battle when the boy was just a toddler.

Elen probably attended the royal women in three locations: Dunfermline, Edinburgh and Linlithgow. She may have been one of the 'More lasses' who were brought, the Lord High Treasurer's accounts tell us, from Dumfermline to Edinburgh in 1504 to escape an outbreak of Plague. She may have been the girl the same accounts tells us was christened there in December 1504 while staying in a merchant's house, after a journey through the Borders with the king. Prior to that naming ceremony, she would not have been Christian. 'More' was not really Elen's surname, and 'Elen' almost certainly not her original name. The word 'More' is most likely a corruption of 'moor', and indicates Elen's African origins.

During the reign of James IV, Europe had begun to look seriously to Africa as a territory to plunder. Portuguese explorers were key to establishing routes, and James licensed Scottish privateers to attack Portuguese ships. One William

Wod was rewarded by the king for bringing him a group of Africans including the 'More lasses'; these people were probably taken from a Portuguese ship. They were variously called 'moors', 'black moors' and 'Ethiopians'; the latter does not necessarily imply that they came from modern-day Ethiopia.

If Elen was taken from a Portuguese ship, she was probably aboard as a slave. At the Scottish court she, her sister and the other 'More lasses' seem to have been valued servants rather than slaves, with good clothes and shoes – double-soled, no less – provided at the king's expense. They received gifts of money and goods from him at key times, such as New Year –once, in 1512, Elen was given five gold French crowns. Descriptions of her garments still exist: in 1506 two 'More lassis', who were probably Elen and Margaret, were given russet-coloured gowns with velvet trimmings and red kirtles – bodices with underskirts attached to wear under a semi-open gown – plus the necessary fabric for linings, stockings and so forth. The next year they were kitted out again, along with one Marjory Lindsay, in gowns embellished with ribbons.

The part Elen played at court was, then, of relatively high status. She was a lady-in-waiting in the inner household of the king's daughter, a role normally taken by a noblewoman or other members of the elite. It is not clear that she was a slave in the sense that she was owned as property, but neither was she realistically able to return home, and her treatment is perhaps suggestive of the way the court might have treated an exotic pet – in fact, the More lasses are listed in a 1504 document with a range of exotic animals also delivered off Wod's ship. Other Black people at court were there to provide entertainment; there was, for example, an African drummer.

On the subject of entertainment, perhaps it was Elen who took her place at the centre of a tournament of 1507 which James called 'the justing of the wyld knicht for the blak lady'. This 'blak lady' was arrayed in serious splendour, with a damask gown adorned with flowers of gold, yellow and green taffeta details and leather oversleeves. She had attendants male and female, and the 'wyld knicht' who fought to defend her honour was no less than King James himself. At one point during the feasting after the tournament, a mechanical cloud descended and 'cleikitt up' the Black Lady, who disappeared from view.

The court poet William Dunbar wrote a piece called 'Ane Black Moir', apparently in response to the tournament. It implies that the 'blak lady' was indeed played by a Black woman, and utilises a range of unpleasant proto-racist imagery to do so. This neatly puts paid to any suggestion that the Scottish court in full and whole saw Elen as entirely human. The poem is not replicated here; it does not deserve to be so.

We do not know when Elen died, but a gift of sixty shillings was made to 'Helenor, the blak moir' in 1527. Perhaps this was Elen, still living at court more than two decades after she arrived.

LIVE YOUR LIFE BY ELEN

There have been people of African origin in Scotland from Classical times, having travelled there with the Roman army. Elen and many other 'Black Moors' appear in court records in the Early Modern period, roughly in line with the beginnings of the trade in African slaves. Scotland would go on to play a significant part in this terrible trade, particularly in the Caribbean, and there was no part of the country innocent of this abuse. Much of the wealth upon which modern Scotland was founded was gained through the exploitation of countless thousands of Black men and women. That the fundamental horror of enslavement was compounded by further depredations such as violence and sexual abuse is also in no doubt. Through abuse, Scots colonists fathered children on their female slaves, others fathered children with free Black women.

Scots colonists returned home with Caribbeans accompanying them: children; servants; slaves. We do not know many of these people's stories in detail but we must not continue the practice of writing them out of our history. As just one example, we might remember the girl of whom Lieutenant Soirle

CONTINUES ON NEXT PAGE

LIVE YOUR LIFE BY ELEN

(Sorley) MacDonald of Skye wrote to his supervisors, requesting permission that she accompany him while fighting in the American War of Independence. She was enslaved. Her name was Doll.

Recently a commentator wrote that ethnic diversity in Scotland was 'patchy at best and in most cases negligible'. This is a deeply problematic statement. Scotland has diverse ethnicity in its DNA. Leaving aside the wave after wave of settlers who sought a life on Scottish soil since prehistory, Scotland has Indigenous Highland Travellers, and other Traveller communities with Romani and non-Romani heritage. Ireland has likewise a large Traveller community, who have been marginalised to the extreme. Ireland also has had a tendency to whitewash its history so that it is, for example, initially jarring to find a reference to a Black man in *Mesca Ulaid*, the Intoxication of the Ulstermen, composed in perhaps the ninth century. Possibly the first arrival of Africans in Ireland was linked to Norse trade in slaves.

In the modern era, migration to Scotland, to Ireland and to Wales continues apace. From the Carribean to Bosnia, Italy to Ukraine, and Poland to Pakistan, many people have left their homes by choice or no choice at all and have found a new home on these shores. They enrich our story; it is their story too and they are 'us'.

ESTHER INGLIS
CALLIGRAPHER, MINIATURIST AND BOOK~MAKER

E sther Inglis was born to French parents in either London or Dieppe in 1571. Her mother was calligrapher Marie Presot, and her father was school teacher and scribe Nicholas Langlois. At an unconfirmed date, Langlois became master of the French School in Edinburgh; the family's decision to relocate to the Scottish capital may have been prompted by persecution of Protestants in France.

From the work Esther undertook over the rest of her life, it is clear that her parents educated her well. She learned her mother's calligraphy skills, and her father had a clear hand in her general learning and in her work on books specifically – her early books contain verses he wrote specially for the purpose. She retained her father's name, after a fashion, in the pen-name she would use for the rest of her life – Inglis, like Langlois, means 'English'.

In 1596 Esther married Bartholomew Kello, who was a clerk at the court of King James VI. Esther herself may have been employed by the king, or at least have used her skills to aid her husband in his work. It seems it was a mutually supportive relationship; Kello proudly signed himself 'husband of the book's adorner' in several of Esther's books, and composed letters and poems to Esther's clients. When he was granted a warrant by James VI, it read that 'the said Barthilmo Kello is to write or cause all the said letters by his discretion be written BY THE MOST EXQUISITE WRITER WITHIN THIS REALM'.

Esther's work is indeed EXQUISITE. She produced richly decorated volumes with gorgeously embellished title pages and borders, entirely copied by hand,

"Both parents having bidden me, a daughter has written, breaking the tedium of exile with her pen."

ESTHER INGLIS
LIVRET CONTENANT DIVERSES SORTES DE LETTRES
1586

although her lettering is so perfect that at first glance the text appears printed. Some of the letters are under a millimetre high. The books were completed by rich bindings embroidered by Esther with perfect skill and precious materials including seed pearls and silver and gold thread. Hand-lettered manuscripts were becoming rarer in the period as printing became more common, and their value was increasing. Esther went for novelty value too, producing books as small as an inch and a half wide by two inches high.

Esther and Kello seem to have hit on a means of marketing Esther's work that capitalised on Kello's royal connections. Essentially, Kello would present the books as lavish gifts while delivering the official documents for which he (and by extension Esther) had been commissioned. These were not sales or commission arrangements exactly, but the hope was that financial recompense would be forthcoming from the recipient. A slightly risky business and the work was high-end stuff. The couple had little choice but to follow the money, moving south of the border when James VI of Scotland became James I of England in 1603.

Kello became Rector of Willingale in Essex, and Esther became more active in presenting her work to its intended audience personally. She often chose to mark significant dates such as New Year; in 1606 no fewer than three grandees received a book from Esther as a gift at this time. These may have been intended not only to extract payment for the 'gift', but also to act as a 'portfolio' by showcasing Esther's calligraphy skills. In the small set of books gifted in 1606, she adopts a new style, decorating each page with flowers, birds or butterflies, using flowered borders and varying the handwriting style on every page.

After 1607, Esther did not produce many more flower-books. That New Year, she chose to bestow a gift on Prince Henry Frederick, King James's eldest son. He was thirteen years old, and Esther made him a book of French religious poems decorated with arms, flowers and fruit. Aside from dedication pages, Esther did not write or commission the text for her works, but copied from existing printed books instead. She often selected religious texts, and somewhat pertly suggested that her choice might be of benefit to the recipient. This apparently did not offend the prince and his retinue; the 1607 gift was the first of a number of books she made for his delight and edification. She gave him a book of Latin Psalms at New Year in 1608, a book of 'Armes' for New Year 1609, and the Psalms in French in 1612, shortly before his death. She was paid the handsome sum of £5 for the 'Armes' and the enormous sum of £22 for the French Psalms.

The large gift may indicate that the prince had become Esther's patron, and she was effectively being paid off after his death. If she was indeed in his employ in this period, it would explain the small number of manuscripts she created between 1607 and 1614 – just eight in total.

Kello and Esther had four children together that we know of. At least two had died before they returned to Edinburgh after 1615. They lived there until Esther's death in 1624. We know of around sixty of her manuscripts in existence today; many of these are held in the most prestigious collections in the world. Her work rarely comes on the market but when it does, it changes hands for sums with which Esther, badass businesswoman, might be quite seriously gratified.

LIVE YOUR LIFE BY ESTHER

Esther paid lip-service to the expectations of her time in terms of female behaviour, for example describing an exquisite gift to a patron as a 'small work of my pad and pen'. In truth she seems to have seen herself as an accomplished artist, linguist, and interpreter of text, signing her work with pride. Her boldness in this regard is not typical of her time, when women were more likely to emphasise their family or matrimonial ties, stick to 'appropriate' subject matter and efface their own personality. She even included self-portraits of herself holding a pen – implying that she saw herself as the creator and not merely the transcriber of books.

Take a leaf from Esther's book and don't fall into the trap of underselling yourself. Some years ago, a Hewlett Packard internal report found that women typically would not apply for a job unless they met 100 per cent of the essential criteria in the job description; men, on the other hand, would apply if they met 60 per cent.

ELIZABETH MELVILLE
LADY CULROSS
POET

I n the heart of Edinburgh, high up in the Old Town in the shadow of the castle, stands Lady Stair's House. It is a fairytale turreted structure with a distinctly Arts and Crafts look deriving from an 1890s restoration that was so concerned with making the house look 'old' that it managed completely to obscure its actual antiquity. Today both house and close are named for Lady Stair, who bought the property in 1719. Prior to that they were named for another woman, Lady Gray, who lived there for many years after her husband built the house in 1622.

While groaning with statues to its own illustrious sons and other great men of the British Empire, Edinburgh is distinctly lacking in memorials to women. Today the house – named in its time for not one but two women – follows that pattern, being home to Edinburgh's Writers' Museum, which celebrates the achievements of Sir Walter Scott, Robert Burns and Robert Louis Stevenson. In 1997, the decision was taken to broaden out this rather narrow male focus, and the area outside the house was earmarked as 'Makar's Court'. The word 'Makar' means 'writer' or 'poet' in Scots.

In 2004, Australian academic and feminist Germaine Greer unveiled a marker in Makar's Court for the first woman writer ever to make it into print in Scotland's history. That woman was Elizabeth Melville, and she was born around 1578, into a Fife landowning family that had endured its fair share of scandal. Her grandfather, John Melville of Raith, had been executed in 1548 on grounds that ultimately derived from his support for the Protestant cause. John's sons – including James, Elizabeth's father – were nonetheless loyal servants to Mary,

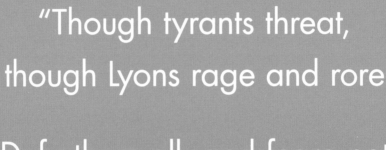

"Though tyrants threat,
though Lyons rage and rore

Defy them all, and feare not
to win out."

ELIZABETH MELVILLE
FROM *ANE GODLIE DREAM*
1606 EDITION

Queen of Scots. They remained loyal to Queen Mary even after her forced abdication, and subsequently served her son, James VI. James Melville married Christian Boswell, daughter of the Laird of Balmuto, who belonged to another family with strong connections to the Stuart court.

Elizabeth Melville was brought up in the family home of Halhill Tower, near Collessie. James had inherited this property from his adoptive father Henry Belnaves, who was in turn a close friend of Scotland's prominent Protestant Reformer John Knox, and Elizabeth would have grown up with the stories of the depredations suffered by these early Protestants ringing in her ears. Clearly she received a good education – perhaps her father was convinced of the value of women's learning by his experience via Mary Stuart of the court in France which, at the time, was presided over by the formidable Catherine de Medici. Elizabeth may also have had access to French poetry in her early years, and perhaps in her mature life too. A glimpse of her personality in her younger days comes from a dedication by the poet Alexander Hume in his book *Hymnes, or Sacred Songs*. He describes her as 'a Ladie, a tender youth, sad, solitare and sanctified', with a gift for the art of 'poesie' in which she 'excelle[d] any of [her] sex'.

Elizabeth's own poetry is strongly informed by her Protestant belief. Her major work, *Ane Godlie Dreame* appeared in print in 1603 and was reissued again and again. It is written in sixty eight-line stanzas with a complex rhyming structure, and details Elizabeth's inner spiritual struggles, along with some daring commentary – given the time and her sex – on church and state. Between its first publication and later reissues, the spelling system changes from Scots to English, and the accompanying matter alters. A shorter poem accompanying the *Dream* in the early editions, 'Away vaine warld', may be by Elizabeth. A 1644 edition contains another piece possibly from her pen, 'Come sweet Lord, my sorrow ceas'.

The *Dream* was a significant success, and eventually there would be twelve editions, that we know of, before it was released for the last time in 1737. It does not seem, however, that any other work by Elizabeth ever appeared in print. She lived towards the end of the era in which hand-written manuscripts were still copied for circulation, and a small number of her poems seem to have reached a readership by this means. As recently as 2002 the scholar Jamie Reid-Baxter identified a sequence of poems and sonnets copied into a manuscript of Edinburgh sermons as Elizabeth's work, based on analysis of the style and content of the verse. He also identified an anonymous poem, 'Love's Lament for Christ's Absence', as by her. It also seems likely that Elizabeth wrote the two stanzas carved into the wall of the mausoleum her father built for her mother in the graveyard at Collessie.

Although not originally written for public consumption, some of Elizabeth's letters have also been published. These reveal something of the circumstances of her marriage to John Colville of West Comrie (or Cumrie), which occurred at some time before 1597. The letters indicate that the couple had seven children, but imply that Colville was not a good husband either in terms of his management of their affairs or of his emotional and spiritual support for Elizabeth and their family. The letters are full of Biblical quotations, advice and humour, but no poetry.

After 1737, Elizabeth's work fell from favour for a time. In the 1800s it began to reappear in anthologies of earlier poetry. It would take another woman, however, to raise Elizabeth's profile in the modern era. Germaine Greer included her poetry in *Kissing the Rod*, Greer's 1988 examination of women's verse from the seventeenth century. This was the link that led to Greer unveiling Elizabeth's marker in Makar's Court in 2004.

LIVE YOUR LIFE BY ELIZABETH

Elizabeth was lucky in that her father, for whatever reason, believed in education for women in an era in which learning opportunities for girls were far from guaranteed. Around the world today, many girls are denied access to education, and many are married unacceptably young, interrupting their education, resulting in early pregnancy with its attendant dangers and leading to increased rates of violence and abuse. If you can, get involved in supporting charities such as Plan UK, which work with communities across the world to end child marriage and promote girls' access to education.

ISOBEL GOWDIE
'WITCH'

I n the middle years of the twentieth century, folklore collecting was serious business in Scotland. Artists like Ewan McColl, Peggy Seeger and her brother Pete, Bob Dylan and more were bringing folk to the masses across the globe, while collectors across the UK and Ireland were frantically attempting to capture centuries-old stories, song and lore from their bearers before the wellspring of tradition ran dry in the face of rapid social change. Collectors at Edinburgh University's School of Scottish Studies hauled their bulky reel-to-reel tape recorders into crofthouses and Travelling camps across the country, recording singers and storytellers whose memory banks of song, story and oral history ran to thousands of hours.

Had Isobel Gowdie lived in the twentieth century, these folklore collectors would have beaten a path to her door. She knew her fairy lore and her charms and incantations, all of which were prized by later collectors. Sadly for Isobel, she lived in the 1600s, and so her command of this rich seam of folklore in fact saw her accused as a witch.

Isobel lived at Loch Loy near Auldearn, just outside Nairn, and it seems she could not read or write. We don't know her date of birth with any certainty; she was married to John Gilbert, a small farmer or farm labourer by 1662, when she made her various confessions. In these, she testified to having been sexually active for some fifteen years, suggesting that she was in her thirties or older. She stated that she helped her husband in his business, selling meat and cloth at market for 'silver (money) and good pryce'.

"I got in in the shape of a jackdaw and Elspet Chisolm was in the shape of a cat. Isobel More was a hare, and Maggie Brodie a cat."

ISOBEL GOWDIE
CONFESSES TO SHAPE~SHIFTING
1662

Isobel and other Auldearn witches were caught up in the last, and most vicious, phase of Scottish witch-hunts. Charles II had just returned to the throne, and perhaps Covenanting landowners wished to crack down on any possibility of renewed confidence amongst those who followed the king's Anglican worship or the Catholicism of his forebears.

Some suggest that Isobel may initially have got herself into trouble with the witch-finders by purposely taunting the minister at Auldearn. We don't know for certain how she came to be accused or to incriminate herself, but we do know that she was interrogated over a six-week period and made four confessions in this time, the first on 13 April 1662. The record says that she wasn't compelled to confess, but this doesn't mean an awful lot. She may have not been tortured by order of the court, which would have meant broken bones, torn-out nails or similar horrors, but she may well have been deprived of sleep, threatened and roughly handled, and was probably kept in solitary confinement in poor conditions. Whether Isobel was subjected to the 'witch-pricking' process – essentially being stabbed over and over with a stout needle or slender blade to find a numb area – is also unclear. There was a witch-pricker active in the area at the time, one John Dickson. Subsequently and surreally it transpired that Dickson was really a woman in disguise, one Christian Caddell. She was later tried for fraud.

If Isobel's confessions were not extracted by torture, it is difficult to know to what they might be ascribed. She describes shape-shifting into the body of a raven and explains the charm for becoming a hare. She testified that she had met Satan in the church at Aldearn at night and even had had sexual intercourse with him – his semen was apparently on the cold side. She and her coven had got up to all sorts of carryings-on including dancing (Dancing! Those early Presbyterians must have been horrified), and interfering with bodies they disinterred. She named her fellow witches but carefully kept her husband out of it – she said she had placed brooms alongside him in bed so he would never know she was gone. She flew about on magical horses, met the Queen of the Fairies whose water-bulls terrified her, and made effigies of the local landowner's children to bring them harm. This aligned with the local landowner's own opinions; he was one of those types who imagine themselves so terribly important in the cosmic scheme of things that any misfortune to befall them must be the doings of the Devil.

All in all, it sounds like Isobel was either giving her interrogators what they wanted, or she was a vivid fantasist. It is possible she was suffering from some form of mental illness, or even under the influence of some form of hallucinogenic. The latter is not without precedent; some witch panics, including the one in which Isobel was accused, are associated with periods after failed harvests. Modern scholarship suggests that a fungus called ergot, which grows on rye in damp conditions, may induce wild hallucinations in those who unknowingly ingest it; we know that Isobel made bread with rye. Of course, there's an outside chance that it was all true and Isobel and friends were having the witchy time of their lives with their cold-semened master and the Fairy Folk, or, at least, carrying out some form of contemporary shamanism involving trance-like states and the performance of charms, incantations and spells to do good and/or evil.

Isobel's later confessions confirm and expand on some of the details of the earlier ones, and introduce some new claims, such as a list of people killed by the coven using elf-shot.

Forty-one people were arrested as a result of Isobel's testimony and that of her fellow coven member, Janet Breadhead. Their interrogators wrote to Edinburgh for permission to try Isobel and Janet; sense did not prevail and Edinburgh gave them the go-ahead. Notes on the confessions indicate that the legal profession was staffed with just as many idiots/misogynists as the kirk and it's associated zealots. One senior lawlord referred to Isobel et al as 'Park's witches', Park being the local landowner. That's right – women can't even be thought of as autonomous beings when they've just finished giving the most memorable confession in the history of Scottish witchcraft.

As with many accused witches, we don't know what happened to Isobel as local records no longer survive. It is likely she was tried and executed at Nairn.

LIVE YOUR LIFE BY ISOBEL

sobel is the first person on record to suggest that a coven was a group of thirteen. The sections of her testimony in which she discusses fornicating with the devil and digging up corpses are admittedly quite out there, but otherwise her coven sounds a little like a group of teens out at night having mildly hysterical, possibly drunken fun. Let's thank our lucky stars that we live in the modern world where we can appreciate our own 'covens' and our ability to draw strength from female friendship.

"The petitioner's husband having deceased within a few years thereafter, leaving young children unfit for the management of such a work, the trust and care of it lay wholly upon the petitioner . . . ever since that time the petitioner had managed the work and advanced the same to a great perfection."

ACT IN FAVOUR OF AGNES CAMPBELL
SCOTTISH PARLIAMENT
1693

AGNES CAMPBELL
PRINTER AND BUSINESSWOMAN

A gnes Campbell was born in 1637 to an Edinburgh merchant couple, Isobel Orr and James Campbell. In 1656, she married Andrew Anderson, a printer to trade. This was a period in which the printing business was changing rapidly. New techniques made printed material ever cheaper, meaning that printers were able to respond to growing demand from the increasing number of people who were able to read. In 1660 Edinburgh's population numbered around 30,000, and the city was beginning to gain a reputation as a centre of artistic and cultural life. This meant there was work to print – and pirated versions of books circulating elsewhere to fall back on if necessary – and readers to buy the resulting products. These were perfect conditions for an enterprising printer, and Anderson was able to build up his business accordingly. In 1663, he was appointed printer to Edinburgh Town Council.

Anderson would go on to build on this success and would be named King's Printer in 1671. This prestigious and lucrative office still exists today; in England and Wales the holder is in receipt of letters patent, granting the exclusive right to publish, license or import the King James Version of the Bible. In Scotland, the office is held by the Bible Board, which in turn licenses a publisher to produce the King James Version.

Andrew Anderson's licence was set for a period of forty-one years, but Anderson only saw out a fraction of this time. He died in 1676, and Agnes took over the licences, eventually joined in the business by her son James. They used these to build the business into the largest printing concern in Edinburgh, but all this careful growth was threatened when Agnes remarried in 1681.

Agnes's second husband was Patrick Telfer, an Edinburgh merchant. Shortly after the marriage, Telfer's affairs fell 'into great disorder' and his creditors turned their eyes to Agnes's wealth. Their argument was essentially that what was hers was his, by her marriage contract or simply by the fact of the marriage itself. Agnes defended this case vigorously; luckily, she had had the foresight to arrange an early-modern version of a pre-nup.

'Tocher' is the Scots word for a dowry, and clever Agnes's tocher came with an iron-clad contract. She had ensured that she brought none of the rights in the printing business and its holdings into the marriage, but rather reserved these for her own use, for any legitimate creditors of Andrew Anderson's, and for her children. Just 10,000 merks fell due to her second husband under this contract – not an insignificant sum, but very far short of the full value of the printing company. Telfer had accepted this deal and had therefore renounced any further rights in the business. His creditors were stymied, but Agnes still had a problem. As a married woman, she could not carry out her business without her husband's say-so. She sought an Act of Parliament 'enabling [her] . . . to acquire and contract in her own name, and pursue and defend, as if she were alone and unmarried'. She succeeded – although the Act passed was specific to Agnes and did not, for example, protect Gwyneth Bebb and her fellow litigants when they attempted to gain the right to practise as solicitors two hundred years later. It was specifically used as an argument against them that a married woman could not contract in her own name (see page 201).

For her part, Agnes was free from the danger that marriage to Telfer had presented, and she continued to manage the business with aplomb. In 1709, she opened the first paper mill on the River Esk, which would go on to become a key Scottish centre for paper production. She was Scottish printer for the works of Daniel Defoe, and was appointed printer to the General Assembly of the Church of Scotland in 1712, around the time the period of her royal licence ran out. In 1704 she purchased the Edinburgh estate of Roseburn and was known as Lady Roseburn thereafter. She died in 1716, leaving a significant fortune to her heirs.

Papermaking on the Esk continued for almost three hundred years after her death.

We know of the milestones of Agnes's career, but less of the bread-and-butter work she must have undertaken in the form of 'little books' (chapbooks) and other mass-market work. Few of these materials printed in Edinburgh in her era survive today, and of those we do have, it is not always possible to say who the printer was. In 1703 and 1708, the City Council decreed that no printer should 'presume to print any papers or pamphlets without affixing their names thereto as printed by them', but not all printers followed this stipulation. Agnes and James did, at least on occasion, mark their work as printed by 'the Heirs and Successors of Andrew Anderson'. Eleven 'little books' marked in this way survive, including catechisms for children, 'godly' books for adults including *Memento Mori* by James Clark and *The Schollars Winter Garment* by Thomas Robins. There was also *The New Art of Thriving*, a small book on household management and economy. For all her business was carried out outside the home, Agnes seems a particularly apt publisher for a book advising women on how to look after themselves after marriage.

LIVE YOUR LIFE BY AGNES

Take a leaf out of Agnes's book (boom boom!) and be smart about legal protections for your property. Keep your records up to date and make a will. If the worst happens, your nearest and dearest will be spared extra administration and uncertainty.

"Their tenets are a strange jumble of enthusiastic jargon; among others she pretends to give them the Holy Ghost by breathing on them, which she does with postures and gestures that are scandalously indecent."

ROBERT BURNS
ON ELSPETH BUCHAN
1782

ELSPETH BUCHAN

'PROPHET'

R obert Burns was not known for being a prude, so it's interesting to speculate just what Elspeth Buchan did to shock him so profoundly when he came across her religious sect in the early 1780s. Perhaps it was spite talking; Burns had an eye on a young lady among the 'Buchanites', and it seems she chose faith over randy Rabbie's advances.

Elspeth Buchan was born in Banffshire in Scotland's north-east in 1738, where her parents Margaret Gordon and John Simpson were roadside inn-keepers. Young Elspeth's early life was marred by her mother's death and thereafter she was farmed out into the care of others. She did not recall this as a happy time, having disliked being put to work and living with scant comfort. A cousin of her mother's educated her in reading and in needlework and intended to take her to the West Indies. Elspeth made the first leg of the journey only, marrying (perhaps unofficially) one Robert Buchan, a potter she met in Greenock. The union was not a happy one, and after various flittings and separations, it ended around 1783. Elspeth then moved to Irvine, having been especially moved by the preaching of Irvine Relief Church Minister Hugh White.

The Hugh White/Elspeth relationship was clearly an odd one, on the intense side by any standards. She wrote to him 'as a friend, not after the flesh, but as a child of another family that has lain in the womb of the everlasting decree from all eternity – a promised seed born from above'. After a short while in her company, White was converted to the idea that she was a saint, and then that she was the Woman Clothed in the Sun from the Revelation of St John. This biblical figure gives birth to a son who is threatened by a dragon. The child goes to Heaven; the woman flees into the wilderness. After a war in Heaven the angels cast out the dragon. The dragon then pursues the woman, who is given wings to escape, and he pours out a great flood that is swallowed by the earth.

As well as believing – or purporting to believe – that Elspeth was this biblical character, Hugh White believed that he was the incarnation of her child. A sermon to this effect saw him promptly deposed from the ministry. Now unwelcome in Irvine but still undaunted, he, Elspeth and their followers followed the Bethlehem Star (or so they said) to a farm outside Dumfries, where they prepared to ascend to Heaven. Elspeth was no fan of marriage and Hugh White had recently returned from America where the charismatic Shaker leader, Amy Lee, had also renounced marriage, although in her case chastity was preferred. Therefore they ran their community along the lines of a free-love commune.

At their height the 'Buchanites' had dozens of members including a number previously of good standing in the community. They lived in communal dormitories, men and women together, and all marriages dissolved.

Elspeth – now known as 'Friend Mother in the Lord' – claimed she could confer immortality by breathing on her followers. The small cult was millenarian; they believed a cataclysmic event was close at hand that would bring about a transformation of the world, perhaps an eventual utopia. This would bring death to many but not their members, who would be taken up in the air to meet Christ. The manner of their transportation involved the shaving of their heads save a topknot – the better to be lifted by the angels – and some fairly extreme dieting. Elspeth retained a full head of hair and forewent the fasting – she needed to keep her strength up, after all.

So-called Doomsday cults with charismatic 'prophetic' leaders are still a feature of modern life. Researchers find commitment to the cult among members even when events foretold by the leader have failed to materialise; this certainly happened with Elspeth's prophecies. In the mould we now recognise, her followers found ways to convince themselves that their leader was still right and the fact that the ascensions failed must have been due to dereliction of some sort on their own part. Today psychologists understand that attempts to dissuade cult members from their beliefs may strengthen the bond; essentially, such attempts play into the narrative that the group are oppressed visionaries. In the modern era, and particularly in societies where firepower is readily available, this has led to a cycle of amplification with tragic results, perhaps most infamously at Waco in Texas.

Elspeth's followers rather had the wind taken out of their sails when Elspeth died in 1791. Nonetheless her power outlived her; one of her followers is reputed to have kept her body unburied until it mummified, awaiting the resurrection she promised him. It never came, but when he died he was buried with her to be on the safe side.

LIVE YOUR LIFE BY ELSPETH (OR RATHER, DON'T)

Perhaps Elspeth's need for attention and adoration derived from the loss of her mother at a young age. While few of us ever feel the need to found our own cult, we can all be insecure, with negative effects on our relationships. If you have trust issues, take ownership of these and work on them, with professional help if you can access it. Make time and space to work things through alone, and allow your partner the same opportunity. Build up your own confidence, and pursue your own interests, to ensure you're bringing positivity to the others in your life.

"Nae militia!"

JACKIE CROOKSTON'S CRY
FROM ORAL TRADITION

JOANNA 'JACKIE' CROOKSTON
PROTESTOR

n 1995 a sculpture was unveiled in Civic Square in the village of Tranent in East Lothian. It is of a type rare in Scotland, because it depicts a named woman. She was Jackie Crookston, and in the statue she marches defiantly along beside a child, her right arm raised with fist clenched, ready to beat the drum she carries.

Jackie was born Joanna Crookston on 12 June 1768 at Gladsmuir. Her birth record lists her parents as 'coalier' James Crookston and his wife Agnes Hogg, and records that the couple baptised their daughter on the eighteenth of June at Gladsmuir Old Kirk. It is thought that Jackie married a man named William Ross around 1789, but the marriage may have been an irregular one as no certificate survives. The couple had more than one child, at least one a son.

Jackie's era was one of heavy losses for British fighting forces in Europe. The Militia Act was passed in 1797 with the aim of replenishing numbers by drawing 6,000 men from ballot in Scotland to serve in the army. This was a deeply unpopular move, proposing as it did to remove working men from poor communities dependent on their labour for economic survival.

The 1790s had seen a spark of defiance lit across Scotland by the French Revolution. No longer were folk content to follow the orders of king and government; rather they hung on the words of radicals such as Thomas Muir. In this spirit, the miners of Tranent were minded to resist conscription. They drew up a proclamation stating their unanimous disapproval of the Militia Act and intention to assist one another in endeavouring to repeal it. They stated that their intents were peaceable, but that coercive measures on the part of the authorities would be viewed as aggression, and answered as such. The document finished, 'Although we may be overpowered in effecting the said resolution, and dragged from our parents, friends, and employment, to be made soldiers of, you can infer from this what trust can be reposed in us if ever we are called upon to disperse our fellow countrymen, or to oppose a foreign foe.'

This proclamation was handed to Major Might, the commanding officer of the recruitment squad in Tranent, on 29 August 1797. It was ignored. A band of protestors went to meet the troops, led by 29-year-old Jackie and her drum, leading the chant of 'nae militia!' Attempts were made to disperse the protest (not, however, to cease the ballot), in response to which Jackie is said to have declared she 'didna care a pin though she were cut in halves, she wad hae nae militia'.

The situation quickly escalated, and the soldiers responded bloodily. Protesters were shot, and a number killed outright. The protesters then fled into the fields around the village, pursued by the Cinque Port Light Dragoons. Accounts said that these soldiers cut down men, women and children indiscriminately, regardless of their level of involvement in the protest. The town subsequently reported pillaging and rape by the dragoons. An official report claimed that their commander Colonel Viscount Hawkesbury, later a British prime minister, was absent and otherwise would have controlled his troops and curtailed these appalling abuses. The events of the day became known as the 'Massacre of Tranent'.

Jackie Crookston's name was not included in the original list of people killed, which numbered eleven. This list was never likely to be complete; there was no great desire on the part of officialdom to formally record the infamous behaviour of the soldiers, nor the names of those who had died in a protest against authority. A contemporary letter by an eye-witness states that six died in the initial confrontation with the soldiers, and that a further fifteen bodies had been found in the fields by the next day, with more protesters still missing. The letter writer speculated that all the bodies would not be found until the corn was cut in the fields at harvest-time. Local tradition has it that he was correct.

There is, then, no official record of Jackie's death. She was a woman, and a poor woman at that, and she died leading a protest against authority. Her family could have recorded her death, but they lived in a time in which a tax was payable for registration of births and deaths, and the passing of many poor people's lives went unmarked as a result. She was remembered instead in the memory of the town she gave her life to defend.

LIVE YOUR LIFE BY JACKIE

Jackie was a radical; she took direct action designed to cause quick change. Today many of us are better at discussing our political beliefs and frustrations online than actually doing anything practical to bring about change. Activism isn't fun; it's hard work. And remember; change cannot happen unless you speak to people who disagree with you. There's no other way to convince them.

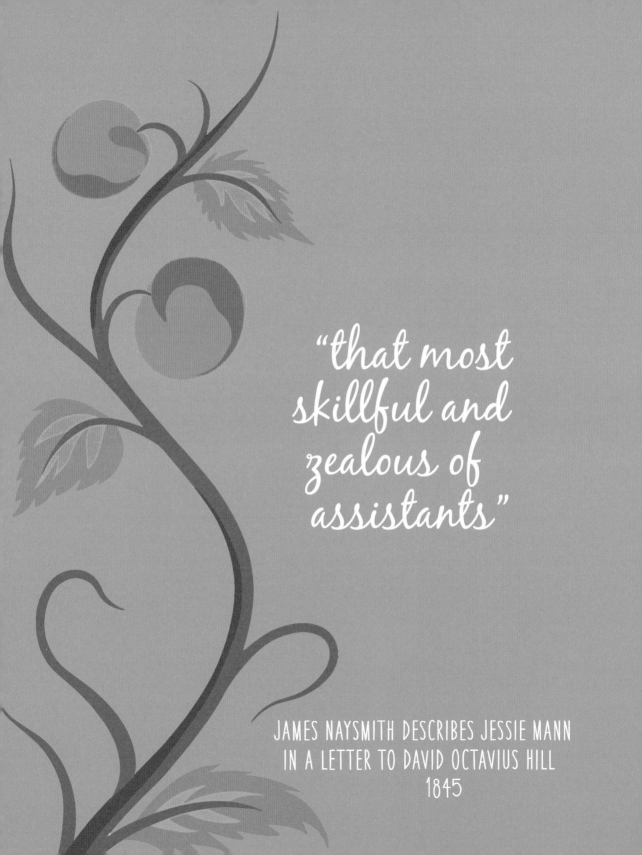

"that most
skillful and
zealous of
assistants"

JAMES NAYSMITH DESCRIBES JESSIE MANN
IN A LETTER TO DAVID OCTAVIUS HILL
1845

JESSIE MANN
PHOTOGRAPHER

The introduction to this book considers the idea of women in the shadows, an image that seems quite apt for Jessie Mann, a pioneer of photography. Jessie was born in 1805, one of the five children of a Perth house painter. When her father died in 1839, Jessie and two of her sisters were unmarried, and the three moved to Edinburgh to live with their solicitor brother, Alexander.

In 1842 Alexander married and his sisters struck out for themselves, moving into a flat in Leopold Place in the Hillside district of east Edinburgh. Hillside sits in the northerly lea of Calton Hill, just over the summit from the site on the south face where early photographers David Octavius Hill and Robert Adamson would set up their studio at Rock House.

Photography was in its infancy in the 1840s. Two alternative processes were introduced in 1839: the daguerreotype, invented by Louis-Jacques-Mandé Daguerre in France, and the calotype, invented in England by William Henry Fox Talbot. The daguerreotype captured an image on a silvered copper plate; the calotype used paper coated in silver iodide. The Scottish scientist Sir David Brewster managed to persuade Fox Talbot not to patent his photographic process outside England and to explain it to Brewster, who had a particular interest in optics. Brewster passed on the steps to his friend Dr John Adamson, who produced the first calotype in Scotland. Adamson then passed the steps on to his brother in turn; by 1842 Robert Adamson was 'well drilled in the art'.

The 1840s were stirring times in Scotland. In 1843 the Church of Scotland split in two with a mass walk-out of ministers from the General Assembly. The painter David Octavius Hill told Sir David Brewster that he wished to paint the dramatic scene; Brewster proposed that he should use photography to capture the likenesses of the ministers present and introduced him to Robert Adamson. Hill and Adamson worked together to take a series of photographs which – years later – Hill would use as the basis for his painting.

Hill and Adamson were a good pairing; Adamson's technical knowledge combined with Hill's abilities in composition and lighting to produce beautiful images that were a world away from the stiffly posed daguerrotypes and calotypes produced previously. They would go on to be a byword for early photography, while a third member of the team would be almost forgotten.

That forgotten person was Jessie Mann, who walked over Calton Hill to work with Hill and Adamson at some point in or before 1845. She was their assistant, and it is probable that her duties extended to taking photographs. In the collection of the National Galleries of Scotland there is a portrait of the King of Saxony taken in Hill and Adamson's studio at a time we know neither was available to have taken it. It is likely that this photograph was taken by Jessie. This would make her not only the first Scottish woman photographer, but one of the first women to take a photograph anywhere in the world. Tate curator Carole Jacobi, who included Jessie in an exhibition of women photographers, says the picture demonstrates that 'she must have been part of their skilful understanding of how you set up a photograph, so she is a real pioneer'.

The team took thousands of photographs in the time they worked together. These included studio portraits of the great and good, photographs of working people, and records of Edinburgh, Fife and the areas around. There is also a photograph thought to be of Jessie herself. She wears a bonnet with flowers and wide white ribbons, and she looks down and out of the frame to her left. One of her hands is stained black, perhaps with silver nitrate from the photographic process. She is a slight, shadowy figure in the exposure, as she has become in the Hill and Adamson story. If this is indeed Jessie, she appears in another photograph, too, with another woman, and Hill placed her in his painting of the Disruption Assembly when he assembled it in 1866.

Hill and Adamson's partnership ended with Adamson's untimely death in 1848. Jessie went to work as a housekeeper in nearby Musselburgh before returning to live with her sister in Edinburgh. She died of a stroke in 1867 and is buried in Rosebank Cemetery in the west of the city.

LIVE YOUR LIFE BY JESSIE

It's tempting to wonder what Jessie might have thought of our modern-day selfie culture. Photographs in her era were historical records and works of art. Now, in our rush to gain 'likes', we can forget that photographs are still a lasting record, and we can forget to live in the moment. Pause for a second and think of Jessie before posting that ill-advised snap or intruding into a private moment in a rush to capture it in pixels.

"'What,' said Lew with some warmth, 'an English clergyman preaching against a Church for which our forefathers have bled and died! How dare he!' So dear Lew did not go back to the church in the afternoon."

ALISON CUNNINGHAM RECORDS THE RELIGIOUS CONVICTION
OF A YOUNG ROBERT LOUIS STEVENSON IN HER DIARY
1863

ALISON CUNNINGHAM

NURSE

A lison Cunningham was born in Torryburn in Fife in 1822 and in 1852 took up post in the house of Thomas and Margaret Stevenson in Inverleith Terrace, Edinburgh, as nursemaid to their son Robert. 'Cummy', as she was known, stayed with the family for twenty years.

Cummy was devoted to the Stevensons and 'Lew', as she called Robert, but her job could not have been an easy one. Robert had inherited the chest problems that ran in his mother's family and regularly suffered with bronchial illness, exacerbated by the chilly, damp rooms of 1 Inverleith Terrace. Cummy nursed him through many long nights of racking coughs, fever, and vivid and awful nightmares. She may have been at least partly to blame for the latter; as a strict Scottish Calvinist she filled Robert's head with fire and brimstone, cautionary religious tales and the bloody history of Scotland's Christian martyrs, and these perhaps fuelled his fevered dreams.

For a period in his childhood, Robert subscribed completely to Cummy's religious views. He later recalled that he had spent a 'Covenanting childhood', reading McCheyne and other Presbyterian authors, and dismissing cards, novels, plays and other entertainments as the work of the Devil. In a diary she kept during a trip to Europe in 1863, Cummy recalled with pride how 'Lew' had come home from the 'English Church' in a great fury after the minister preached against the Presbyterian belief to which she – and through her, her young charge – were devoted.

As he grew to adulthood, Robert Louis Stevenson did not maintain Cummy's strict Christian doctrine; instead, he was both to relinquish his Christian faith and to become one of the most famous novelists in the world. But Cummy's early influence remains clear in his work, which is packed with the intrigues and excitement of Scotland's past, and horrified fascination with ideas of good and evil. He wrote twice in the Scots language – the classic stories *Thrawn Janet* and *The Tale of Tod Lapraik* – and perhaps Cummy's influence is clearest there, since she must have had a 'guid Scots tongue in her heid', and a working knowledge of the traditional beliefs and fears of the Scottish countryside.

Stevenson travelled far from Scotland in his later years, but Cummy was not far from his mind. He wrote to her from France in 1883, apologising for being 'one of the meanest rogues in creation' for neglecting her. In his letter he told her that he had written a collection of rhymes for children, and had dedicated it to Cummy. 'This little book,' he wrote, 'which is all about my childhood, should indeed go to no other person but you, who did so much to make that childhood happy.' The book was *A Child's Garden of Verses* and is still read and loved the world over today. It contains the poem 'The Land of Counterpane,' recalling a childhood spent in illness, and in the dedication Stevenson acknowledges all the loving care he received from Cummy:

To Alison Cunningham
from her Boy

For the long nights you lay awake
And watched for my unworthy sake:
For your most comfortable hand
That led me through the uneven land:
For all the story-books you read:
For all the pains you comforted:
For all you pitied, all you bore,
In sad and happy days of yore.

Cummy outlived her charge by some margin. Stevenson died in 1894 at just forty-four years old, and was buried in Samoa. Cummy lived until 1913 and enjoyed many chances to talk about her time with 'Lew' as the popularity of *A Child's Garden of Verses* conferred a modest celebrity upon her. When she died at ninety-two, Stevenson's widow Fanny paid for a memorial stone for her grave in Morningside Cemetery in Edinburgh. In its infinite wisdom Edinburgh City Council knocked this marker down in the early 2000s, citing safety concerns. There was outcry from fans of Stevenson and the marker was reinstated.

LIVE YOUR LIFE BY CUMMY

In Stevenson's era, books for children were considered serious business. Today we live in another golden age for children's books, but this branch of literature – beyond Harry Potter – is often dismissed as offering nothing 'for grown-ups'. Do yourself a favour and dip into a children's title now and then. From classics like the Moomins to modern picture-book legend Jon Klassen or storytelling maestro Philip Pullman, there is serious joy to be found on the children's shelves of your local bookshop or library.

"after my first success
I could not sleep with
excitement"

PHOEBE ANNA TRAQUAIR
DESCRIBES THE JOY OF DISCOVERING A NEW MEDIUM
1910

PHOEBE ANNA TRAQUAIR

ARTIST

Phoebe Anna Moss was born on 24 May 1852, the sixth of the seven children of a doctor and his wife in Kilternan, County Dublin. She studied art initially in Ireland, at the Royal Dublin Society, where she was tasked with illustrating fossil fish for a young Scottish palaeontologist, Ramsay Heatley Traquair, who was keeper of the Society Museum. Phoebe and Ramsay went on to marry in 1873, and relocated to Scotland, setting up home in Colinton, where their three children Ramsay, Harry and Hilda were born.

Phoebe's early years in Edinburgh saw her focus on watercolours and embroidery. She was greatly influenced by Rosetti, whose work her brother William collected, and by the work of the visionary poet-painter William Blake. Ultimately she would become a shaping force on the Arts and Crafts movement and Scotland's Celtic Revival in her own right, working in a range of techniques from illuminated manuscripts to enamelling.

In 1885, the Edinburgh Social Union gave Phoebe her first professional commission, engaging her to decorate a tiny chapel at Edinburgh's Hospital for Sick Children with murals. Phoebe transformed the formerly dark structure – it had been a coalhouse – with a glowing mix of Celtic, Byzantine and pre-Raphaelite imagery, creating a chapel of rest that aimed to offer some comfort to bereaved parents. The work was completed in 1886, but the hospital moved from its original location of Lauriston Lane to its iconic site at Sciennes only ten years later. Phoebe campaigned for the preservation of the murals and oversaw the transfer of all elements that could be moved. She then repaired and extended the scheme.

Phoebe's second major public commission was for the Song School at St Mary's Cathedral. Here she was inspired by a hymn to celebrate Creation. In the work she reflects on the importance of the arts, incorporating portraits of poets, artists and writers, alongside the choristers of the cathedral and the clergy there.

The Song School raised Phoebe's profile enormously. She was approached to decorate the entrance hall of the Scottish National Portrait Gallery, but turned down this opportunity in favour of another commission from the Edinburgh Social Union, for a vast series of murals in the Catholic Apostolic Church on Mansefield Place in Edinburgh. We now have glimpses of the way she worked – not from her own account but from lectures and articles by the movers and shakers of Edinburgh's art world. James Caw, Director of the National Gallery of Scotland, tells us she did not use preparatory sketches, but 'wrought direct upon the walls . . . she waits until an idea shapes itself in colour and line in her mind's eye, and then transfers it to the walls at once, thus retaining the vividness and freshness.' She diluted her oils with turps and beeswax in order to give a glow and translucency on the white base she applied over the plaster. The finished murals were varnished and then buffed gently with beeswax and turpentine to give a silky sheen. She also applied metal leaf and raised areas with gesso and string.

Before Mansefield Place, Phoebe was a regular contributor to national Arts and Craft exhibitions; the new murals made her name the world over. It seemed the world was at her feet, but the old spectre of sexism raised its head and she was turned down for membership of the Royal Scottish Academy. She was made an honorary member in 1920, but the first woman associate member would not be allowed to join for another eighteen years after that.

In her later years, Phoebe travelled extensively, visiting India, North Africa and the Mediterranean. Her eyesight began to fail in the 1920s and she produced very little work after 1925. She died in 1936 and was buried with her husband in Colinton Churchyard, with a stone she herself designed. It lists her membership of the Royal Scottish Academy, reminding us of the importance of those endorsements from which women of her era were routinely excluded.

Phoebe's work fell out of fashion after her death, as Modernism prompted a rejection of the embellished and traditional. She was quite neglected as an artist until the 1990s, when her exquisite work was reconsidered and museums and galleries scrambled to acquire her pieces. At this time her murals at

Mansefield Place were in danger of complete destruction as the building had fallen into disrepair and much of the plaster had suffered water damage. An enormous voluntary effort saw the monies raised for a thirty-month restoration and the murals now form the centrepiece of a glorious events venue and a hub for charitable organisations.

LIVE YOUR LIFE BY PHOEBE

From embroidery to enamelling, Phoebe practised a lot of applied art and craft. Women's work of the past is often of this type, and tends to be dismissed as a result, with 'serious' disciplines (= open only to males) of fresco, oil painting and sculpture considered 'proper art'. Don't buy into this snobbery; there are a lot of bad oil paintings out there, and a lot of gorgeous tapestry. You'll be in good company; Turner Prize winner Tracey Emin has taken the sampler and the quilt and made them her own.

"Headed by a band of improvised instruments, including tin whistles, hooters, and a huge drum, the procession aroused a good deal of interest. The majority carried large placards with the words: 'Rent Strikers. We're not Removing'."

THE GOVAN PRESS DESCRIBES THE RENT STRIKE
LED BY MARY BARBOUR
NOVEMBER 1915

MARY BARBOUR
POLITICAL ACTIVIST

Like Joanna Crookston (see page 53), Mary Barbour is one of the very few Scottish women immortalised with a statue. Hers stands at Govan Cross in Glasgow and is the result of the efforts of the Remember Mary Barbour Association, formed to address both the lack of a proper memorial to a heroine of political activism, and the chronic shortage of memorials to women in Scotland more generally.

Mary Rough was born in Kilbarchan in Renfrewshire in 1875. Her father was a carpet weaver and Mary initially trained as a thread twister and then a carpet printer. She married journeyman iron turner David Barbour in 1896, and set up home with him in Elderslie. Their firstborn David arrived in December of the same year, and the small family moved to Dumbarton where poor wee David contracted meningitis and died in October 1897. This was long before vaccines were available for the disease, or antibiotics to tackle its bacterial form. In its viral form it is hugely infectious and liable to spread rapidly in overcrowded accommodation. Perhaps this tragedy informed Mary's lifelong commitment to housing and healthcare for all.

Mary's second son, James, was born in Dumbarton before the family moved again, to Govan, where her third son William was born. Govan was a deeply deprived area, and Mary quickly became involved with various organisations campaigning for change. She joined the Socialist Sunday Schools, a nationwide movement promoting reform by educating children in the causes and effects of poverty, and the Scottish Co-operative Women's Guild. The Guild campaigned for policies to address women's poverty, including maternity benefit, education, the right to vote and a national minimum wage. The Guild trained its members in political organisation and running, chairing and addressing political meetings. Armed with this new political education, Mary also became a member of the Independent Labour Party, heavily active in what was to become known as 'Red Clydeside'.

Despite the efforts of Mary and her contemporaries in pre-war socialist movements, the outbreak of the First World War saw conditions in Govan deteriorate further. Thousands of workers were pressed into service in munitions, in the shipyards and in other war-related manufacturing activity, and these individuals had to be housed alongside the existing population. As conditions worsened, rents actually rose as unscrupulous landlords saw an opportunity to take advantage of government mobilisation orders by overcharging for the already overcrowded accommodation available, in this way hoping eventually to evict poorer tenants to make way for the comparatively wealthier munitions workers.

In 1914 the Glasgow Labour Party Housing Committee and the Women's Labour League set up the Women's Housing Association or WHA to protest rent exploitation. In 1915 Mary was a founder member of the South Govan WHA. The Association claimed many members among women who had not been politically active previously but were moved to action by the landlords' greed. The women refused to pay inflated rents, and worked together to support and help those threatened with eviction as a result. They met in Govan's closes to share intelligence and rang hand-bells and rattles to gather crowds to repel Sherriff's officers sent to enforce evictions. Shipyard and factory workers threatened strikes in support of the women, many of whom had husbands, sons and other family members fighting at the Front.

On 17 November 1915, thousands of women, shipyard and engineering workers converged on the Sherriff Courts in Ingram Street to protest eighteen forthcoming evictions. They were known as 'Mrs Barbour's Army' and were joined by other key figures in the Red Clydeside movement, including the radical John MacLean. The crowd was peaceably broken up, but not before Sherriff Lee, inside the court, had advised the landlords' agents to drop their actions ahead of an enquiry into the matter. Munitions minister David Lloyd George was notified, and a month later Parliament passed the Rent Restrictions Act, limiting rent at pre-war levels for the duration of the war and six months thereafter. This was a turning point in housing history in Glasgow and across the world as many cities followed suit in introducing rent control.

Mary now turned her attention to the anti-war movement. She and her friends Helen Crawfurd and Agnes Dollan orchestrated a campaign of leafleting, protest and civil disobedience from 1916 until the end of the war. Her organisational skills were recognised in 1920, when she was selected to stand for election as a councillor. Women's suffrage helped her into office, as one of the first women councillors in Glasgow. She was subsequently appointed Bailie of the City of Glasgow in 1924, the first woman to hold the office, and also one of the city's first women magistrates. For the remainder of her political career she retained a staunch commitment to women and children's healthcare, advocating for the provision of child welfare services, free school milk and children's playgrounds. She served on committees working to end mortality in childbirth and – controversially among her Independent Labour Party colleagues – to gain access to birth control for women. She also worked to establish municipal wash-houses and bring about an end to slum housing. In her own words, she pushed, 'not only for better homes, but for a higher standard of living generally'.

Mary died at the age of eighty-three in 1958.

LIVE YOUR LIFE BY MARY

As well as the statue in Govan Cross, Mary's achievements have been marked in recent years with the Mary Barbour Prize for women bringing about change in Glasgow.

Remembering women is important, and it doesn't happen enough. Be an advocate for prizes named after women, statues of women, trains named after women, women on banknotes and any other opportunities you see to honour our foremothers.

IRELAND

BOLD HUSSIES AND CAILÍNS AND SEAFARING QUEENS

PRE-HERSTORY

The first evidence of prehistoric peoples in Ireland dates from around 10,500 BC, when a small population of hunter-gatherers lived a nomadic life on the island. In the Neolithic era (from c. 4,000 BC), the introduction of agriculture saw the development of complex, settled societies which built megalithic tombs and other monuments, often astronomically aligned. Evidence of Neolithic cultivation exists, too, preserved under blanket peat.

In the Copper and Bronze Ages (from c. 2,600 BC), Ireland became a centre for metalworking including goldsmithing – male-default thinking tends to have it that metalsmiths were men without any particular evidence to that effect. Crannogs were built – houses on stilts in water – and the remains of great cauldrons and meat-hooks suggest that feasting was important.

We do not know precisely when Celtic-language speakers reached Ireland, but by the Iron Age (c. AD 500) we can say with some certainty that Ireland's culture was Celtic. Ring-forts proliferated and trade took place across the Irish Sea and further afield. This may have included trade in slaves.

The great epic stories of Irish mythology come to us via later writers, but purport to date from this time and probably draw on early sources. Women appear as queens, as warriors and trainers of warriors, and as wisewomen, possibly drawing on half-remembered traditions of female deities. Queen Medb causes a war with a cattle-raid. The women of Ulster hold a (literal) pissing contest atop tightly packed stacks of snow. Macha is made to race against a chariot while heavily pregnant with twins; she curses the warriors of Ulster and they suffer her labour pains.

We cannot say for certain to what degree goddesses were worshipped or queens reigned in reality because, in line with much of the rest of the world, kingship gradually came to be the locus of power in Ireland. To attain and retain kingship, success in battle was key, and such female power as there had been gradually waned.

EARLY HERSTORY

Male-centric society was fertile ground for the introduction of Christianity, and various missions spread the belief across Ireland from the fifth century AD onwards. The Latin written record tells of the establishment of monasteries, the missions of Irish figures into other countries, and the gradual Christianisation of the country. A strong tradition of visual art combined Pagan and Christian imagery to great effect, reaching its pinnacle in the Book of Kells.

Women are not absent from early Christian Ireland; some priests and monks of the era had wives, and women played their own part in the spread of the faith. One key female figure was Brigid of Kildare, an early Irish nun. Some of the worship of Brigid may draw on beliefs of the pre-Christian Celtic goddess Brìd, with whom she shares a name. She lived – if she was indeed a historical character – in the fifth century AD. Biographies of Brigid credit her with establishing religious life for Irish women, founding religious houses and establishing a school of art. All of this suggests that women could have been rather more involved in the high achievements of the early Irish church than the record has given them credit for.

INVASIONS

Ireland's stability and cultural confidence were undermined just before AD 800 by Viking raids (a new study suggests that women too sailed in Norse raiding parties but previously male-default thinking has determined all graves containing weaponry to be male). In the two centuries of warfare that followed, many Irish people – including women – were taken into slavery. A key measure of success for Irish kings was repelling the invaders, but fighting between Irish kingdoms fractured resistance and offered the Vikings fertile ground for fresh forays. The Norse invaders began to settle in Ireland, building towns and cities and eventually intermarrying with the native Gaelic population.

Having helped conquer England in 1066, Norman lords were set on capturing territory to the west and invaded Ireland in 1169. Afraid of the establishment of rival interests to his own, Henry II of England invaded in 1171. Many Irish kings agreed to acknowledge Henry, perhaps because they hoped he would function as a sort of absentee high king, allowing them to continue to pursue their own aims in peace. In fact, Norman barons seized large swathes of land, administering these almost as kingdoms in their own right. But gradually the Irish order reasserted itself, aided by the Black Death, by famine, and by involvement of the English monarchy in military and land campaigns elsewhere. The Hiberno-Normans' control of Ireland slipped and they retreated within 'the Pale' – the area surrounding Dublin. Elsewhere Gaelic culture was again in the ascendant and even those Normans who remained in Ireland adopted Irish culture. Eventually the *Sean-Ghaill*, or 'Old English', became so Gaelicised that the parliament in the Pale attempted to make it illegal for anyone born in England to speak Irish, wear Irish clothes or marry an Irish person.

While Gaelic Ireland was a patriarchal society and men and women were not fully equal, women had rather better rights than in many parts of Europe. The Brehon legal system required permission from both partners for marriage, divorce was permitted and women could own property and govern land in their own right. A key female figure of the early Norman era who illustrates this is Aoife, daughter of Leinster king Diarmait Mac Murchada. Aoife married Richard 'Strongbow' de Clare, Earl of Pembroke, the leader of the Norman invasion. After Aoife's husband died, she retained a lifetime interest in their land, and defended it by military means as required.

Gaelic Ireland again faced significant challenge in the Tudor era. In 1542 King Henry VIII was declared King of Ireland, and over the next sixty years, English power was consolidated across the country. For a time Irish leaders largely operated as they had always done – Gráinne Ní Mháille was one (see page 103) – but gradually Tudor military might and landgrabs undermined the system. Eventually Ireland would be fully conquered and 'planted' with Protestant settlers.

Irish involvement in failed wars fought in support of the exiled James II (James VII of Scotland) were followed by the introduction of harsh Penal Laws, which significantly reduced the rights of Catholics in public life and land ownership. Some 95 per cent of Irish land ultimately ended up in Protestant hands and much of the population was reduced to abject poverty, starving under absentee landlords while the country produced an abundance of food for export at profit. Several armed rebellions were violently put down. During the 1700s Ireland was a theoretically autonomous kingdom with its own parliament; in fact it was effectively a client state controlled from London. By 1800 the Acts of Union had been passed, formally annexing Ireland to the United Kingdom from 1801.

FAMINE

The period immediately after Union was one of increasing industrialisation, with factory production established in industrial regions across Europe. This affected the textile industry, which had previously been key to Irish women in the form of piece-work completed in their homes. Payment was poor, but might just supplement other income enough to make the difference between sinking and swimming. With the exception of the north-east of Ireland, this income was not replaced by factory work for women as happened elsewhere, and the result for many was extreme economic fragility. This made these women and their families especially vulnerable when the Great Famine struck.

The Famine saw mass starvation and disease savage Ireland in the years between 1845 and 1849. Twenty per cent of the population was lost; around one million people to starvation and disease and a further million to emigration. The death toll was one of the greatest anywhere in Europe in the nineteenth century.

The trigger for the Famine was failure of the potato crop due to blight, but the scale of the disaster was due to a long history of policy failure. Absentee English and Anglo-Irish landlords farmed out rent collection to (often unscrupulous) middlemen. Tenants had no rights and little opportunity or incentive to improve their land. Under the hideously titled 'Popery Act', land held by Roman Catholics had to be subdivided among the owner or (usually) tenant's sons on death. This had resulted in a huge number of tiny smallholdings on which potatoes were the only crop that could support a family. This single-crop dependency represented very serious food insecurity. Meanwhile, the richest land was used to pasture landowners' cattle for sale overseas.

As the disaster unfolded, opportunities to halt its spread were missed. Early indications of blight were ignored until the crop was lifted; this delayed the provision of alternatives to the failed potatoes. Repeal of harsh corn taxes and programmes of food-aid and other relief were half-hearted, stop-start or lacking entirely. Essentially, government and landowners failed to grasp the scale of the disaster, and many simply did not care. Even as charitable collections began to pick up pace, export of livestock, ham, bacon, peas, beans, onions, salmon and other foodstuffs *from* Ireland continued.

As a touching footnote to the horror, members of the American Choctaw First Nation sent a donation to help, less than twenty years after they too had faced displacement, starvation and disease on the Trail of Tears. Irish President Mary Robinson commemorated this act in 1995.

In the years after the Famine, emigration proceeded apace as the Irish population sought a better standard of living than could be achieved in Ireland. Young, unmarried women made up a significant percentage of migrants. Whether they left by choice or not, these women would have enjoyed greater autonomy than those remaining at home, where the choice was often a husband chosen by one's parents, or to remain unmarried at home.

The fortunes of Irish migrants to the New World were mixed. Louisa May Alcott, author of the beloved classic *Little Women*, wrote a blast against 'foreign incapables' in 1874. It seems Alcott – recorded in history as a feminist and an abolitionist – could not see past the 'faults of the race' in the case of 'Biddies', as she called Irish women. 'No Irish Need Apply' appeared in hundreds of American job adverts of the time.

Famine raised its head again in Ireland in 1879. By then the Land Wars were underway as various Land Leagues sought tenants' rights and rent relief. Tensions within this movement spilled over into Nationalist politics as the independence movement gained momentum.

HOME RULE AND INDEPENDENCE

Irish politicians had been seriously calling for Home Rule since the 1880s. This was finally granted in 1912 but was quickly undermined by paramilitary Unionist action in the north. In 1913 the legislation was finally passed, with Ulster partitioned from the remainder of Ireland, but this was suspended in response to the breakout of the First World War. War divided Home Rule campaigners. Some argued that Ireland should fight with Britain; others prepared for revolt.

The Easter Rising of 1916 did not enjoy extensive popular support, but harsh British reprisals in the aftermath galvanised support for independence. The key female leader of the Rising – 'Countess' Constance Marckiewicz – escaped execution on the basis of her sex. Constance stood for election in 1918 on a pro-independence and anti-conscription ticket, and was elected as part of an electoral landslide for Sinn Féin. She never took her Westminster seat; Sinn Féin instead formed a breakaway government in early 1919 and declared an Irish Republic. A violent War of Independence erupted, brought to an end in 1921 by the Anglo-Irish Treaty, which provided for an Irish Free State within the Commonwealth, and for the partition of Ireland to allow six counties in the north-east to opt out and remain within the UK. Civil war followed between those who supported the Treaty – at least as a stepping stone to a full Republic – and those who considered it betrayed those ideals. The Treaty supporters won, and the republic did eventually come. In 1937 the Constitution of Ireland replaced the Free State with the state of Éire, and in 1949 the country became a constitutional republic.

The struggle for Irish independence often overlapped with the women's suffrage movement. Some female campaigners feared that independence would be prioritised over women's suffrage, but James Connolly and others emphasised equality between the sexes. Thousands of members of Cumann na mBan (the Women's Association) fought alongside their brother Republicans in the Rising. Many women took seats in the new legislature, facilitated by full citizenship; often these were widows, sisters and daughters of powerful men. Older women who had never married or had been freed from the bonds of marriage by widowhood were quite the force to be reckoned with. This political equality did not, however, usher in a new era of women's rights; instead married women were barred from public service and teaching in national schools, and all women from various other classes of employment. Contraception was banned.

Up to and beyond the Free State, continuing emigration helped make for a slightly better standard of life for those who remained in Ireland, both by sending home funds, and by relieving overcrowding, but working-class women's lives remained back-breakingly hard. For many, access to piped water, gas and electricity would not arrive until the middle years of the twentieth century. Middle-class households received these conveniences much earlier, and those women eased the burden by taking on other women, and particularly girls, as domestic servants. This practice lasted much longer in Ireland than in the UK and elsewhere in Europe. Finally the supply of domestic servants dried up from the 1940s onwards, as another mass wave of emigration saw women begin to travel to the UK to find work. The marriage rate dropped in Ireland, as women were forced to chose between marriage and employment and picked the latter. Among those who did marry, families tended to the large, but significant improvements in mother and baby care reduced maternal mortality and the burden on families of the care of motherless infants.

After the partition, as before, conditions in Ulster were a little easier but segregation along sectarian lines saw the Troubles begin in the 1960s. Women were a key force in the Civil Rights movement during the period and women – within Ireland and elsewhere – played a vital part in bringing the Troubles to an end.

Large-scale social change from the 1960s saw married women in the Republic able to work in a wide range of occupations, and a stimulated economy in both urban and rural contexts, supported by Ireland's membership of the EU. Female attendance at university soared in the 1970s; the number of women following a religious vocation began to fall in the same decade. Women were admitted to the police force (the Gardaí) and to the armed forces. In 1990 Mary Robinson become Ireland's first female president; she was followed by Mary McAleese in 1997.

In recent years, exposure of misogynistic abuse by the Catholic Church of 'immoral women' in the Magdalene Laundries and other Mother and Baby homes has given momentum to campaigns for equality. These have included an Equal

Marriage referendum and a referendum on the 8th Amendment, which barred access to termination of pregnancy. These have been watershed moments for many women in Ireland in beginning to come to terms with significant harms perpetrated over many generations.

As you read on, bear in mind the long and significant history of discrimination and challenge Irish women have faced. Against this backdrop, the achievements of the amazing Irish women whose stories follow are even more awe-inspiring. As Mary Robinson said, the women of Ireland, 'instead of rocking the cradle, rocked the system'.

"To have the bog dug down into, and examined, was what appeared the only method left to gain information."

PARTICULARS RELATIVE TO A HUMAN SKELETON
BY THE COUNTESS OF MOIRA
1785

DRUMKEERAGH WOMAN
AND
ELIZABETH
LADY MOIRA
SUBJECT AND SCIENTIST

We can't really say that Drumekeeragh Woman was badass. In fact, we know almost nothing about her: not her name; not her age; not how she died. We can't even say for certain that she *was* a woman. We might not remember her at all, were it not for another woman, who lived many hundreds of years after Drumkeeragh Woman died and most certainly rocked the system.

Drumkeeragh Woman was one of a group of eerily preserved human remains known as bog bodies. Her corpse was discovered in a small bog near Drumkeeragh in County Down in 1780, by a local man cutting turf (peat) for his fire. The body was clothed and had long hair, in plaits of just under a foot and a half long.

Today we understand that the conditions in peat bogs are such that bodies buried there may be naturally mummified. Bogs are acidic, cold and low in oxygen, and when a body is lowered into this environment, flesh and hair may be preserved, tanned dark in colour in the case of skin, and red in the case of hair. Some bog bodies have been so well preserved that their fingerprints may be taken. Bones and teeth may be dissolved or degraded by the acid in the bog, as may some metals, and some fibres fare better than others. In fens and some other bog types on the other hand, skeletons tend to be preserved and flesh not. As well as bodies, bogs yield other organic matter on occasion, such as vellum books or containers of butter (yum!). It is not clear whether people buried their booty in the understanding that it would be preserved for later retrieval, or whether they intended to leave items in the bog for good, aware or unaware of the preservative powers of the peat.

Why bodies were buried in bogs is a complex question. These burials span a huge geographical territory, from Denmark to Poland, and happened over many thousands of years. Most belong to the Iron Age (reckoned at 800 BC to AD 150 in the UK and Ireland), but the oldest we know of dates from 8,000 BC; and both more modern formal and accidental burials have also taken place in peat bogs. In Ireland the oldest fleshed body (as opposed to a skeleton) dates from 2,000 BC. For a time the bodies were treated as one group and archaeologists focused on commonalities in their analysis of the bodies' secrets.

The Iron Age bodies do tend to have one specific thing in common – few died of old age in their beds.

Instead, these people were strangled, stabbed, bludgeoned or sometimes 'over-killed' by a combination of all three, leading experts to speculate that they were executed criminals, or human sacrifices. The latter explanation has been favoured on the basis of the apparently high status of a range of the bodies. This is indicated by fine clothing, jewellery or other ornamentation, by manicured nails and soft hands that appear unused to manual labour, or by stomach contents including meat and traded goods that would have been luxuries at the time. Some suffered from scoliosis, bone issues or other disabling conditions and may have been marked out as 'different' in this way.

Increasingly archaeologists and scientists accept that there is unlikely to be one explanation that neatly fits a body found in Denmark and one in Ireland, another in Germany and one in Poland. In Ireland, a new theory emerged in the 2000s that bog bodies may be deposed kings, offered as sacrifice or killed as punishment for failing their people in some way. This is based on plotting their locations against known boundaries of king lands, on the apparently high status of the individuals involved, and on specific mutilations – brace yourself – to the nipples. The theory goes that a king's nipples were suckled as part of a fealty ceremony and specifically destroyed on the king's death to show he had fallen. (Note: if you are ever awarded an OBE or invited to a royal garden party, don't even try to get near any royal chest area.)

Counter arguments maintain that these are interpretations at best, based on observation of imperfectly preserved matter which provides significant challenge even to the latest science. In some cases of 'over-killing', for example, new interpretations have argued that original post-mortem examinations underestimated the potential for bone damage caused by the pressure of the bog. In the case of the Irish 'kings', it may be that the delicate tissue of the nipples was destroyed post-mortem by acids in the bog.

Whether the bodies were sacrificial victims or executed criminals, failed rulers or outcasts, a range of the above dependent on their location, or something else entirely, it is hard to argue against the idea that bogs themselves were important to the people who placed the bodies there. Bogs may have been 'other', outside the known world where people lived – this might explain why criminals or disgraced people were placed there. There may have been a belief in gods or goddesses in the bogs, or that the bogs themselves *were* gods and goddesses, which is in line with the sacrifice theories, and other practices which saw precious metals and other objects apparently 'given' to the bog.

Most of the bog bodies we know of were found after 1800. Drumkeeragh Woman was an early discovery. She attracted a lot of attention, and the best items of her clothing were taken for use by local people (waste not, want not). Even today, preserving bog bodies once unearthed is a challenge; back then there was no way to do it. By the time Drumkeeragh Woman came to the attention of local landowner Elizabeth Rawdon (née Hastings), Countess of Moira, she had already been reburied, with the exception of a plait of hair and some small bones adhered to fragments of rough cloth. The remnants of her possessions had been much abused and eventually scattered back over the bog. Nonetheless Elizabeth determined to get her hands on everything she could.

Elizabeth was an impressive character. She was the daughter of the dreadfully named Theophilius, the 9th Earl of Huntingdon and his wife Selina Shirley, an enthusiastic evangelist who founded her own religious denomination. In addition to the lands of her husband the Earl of Moira, Elizabeth inherited five baronies in England in her own right on her brother's death. She used her wealth and influence as a patron of the arts and an antiquarian; her intention with regard to the bog body was to investigate it scientifically. She published her findings in 1785 in the journal *Archaeologica*, giving us the first ever documented scientific consideration of the phenomenon.

Elizabeth described the body's skeletonised condition, its west–east alignment and, taking into consideration a previous turf-cutting, a calculation that it lay eleven feet deep in the bog. She noted that it lay on gravel, with a stone near its head and various garments about it. She considered its diminutive size to indicate that it was probably – though not definitively – the body of a woman.

Elizabeth considered the possibility that the body was that of a famine victim around the time of the Tudor conquest of Ireland. She was keen to study its garments, since suppression of native Irish culture had made such things rare, and prevailed upon the finder of the body to buy back such pieces as he could. These included very fine fragments, and certain colours – or rather certain discoloration – indicated to her that perhaps metal had also been present in the burial. When she questioned the finder on this count, however, she scared him off, since the poor man thought he was being accused of stealing buried treasure. Elizabeth then determined to dig into the peat, in the hope of finding other burials.

She was disappointed in this hope, but did find various pieces of textile which she attemped to place in her article within the history of Irish and broader European Celtic apparel as she understood it. She thought that many of the textiles had originated outside Ireland. She was surprised to find no linen and, although she was working without reference to the extensive bank of information on bogs and bog bodies available today, she was still able to reach the – probably correct – conclusion that this had rotted away. She found visual references for the plaits in the hair (there originally were two but one was lost) in continental sources.

Elizabeth concluded that the body was of considerable antiquity, and had been purposely buried within some structure that had disintegrated, leaving behind the gravel-like substance the finder described. Based on her observations of the cloth, understanding of the history of the area and previous archaeological finds, she considered there might be a link to 'druidical' ceremony or rites of justice. She concluded the body might be that of a Danish invader in the ninth century, or an Irish prince or royal female expediently buried during a period in which native power was suppressed by invaders.

Elizabeth understood the limitations of what she called her 'mutilated and conjectural' account, acknowledging that there were issues with all of her theories. Since Drumkeeragh Woman's body no longer survives, we cannot use modern techniques such as radiocarbon dating or isotope analysis to determine more of her story. Some modern commentators consider that she was a considerably more recent burial than Ireland's Iron Age bog bodies, and probably post-medieval. This does not explain who she might have been and what she was doing in that place, under eleven feet of peat and with no suggestion of a graveyard nearby.

LIVE YOUR LIFE BY DRUMKEERAGH WOMAN AND ELIZABETH

The science of bog bodies is not necessarily something you might immediately say was for you, but neither was it obviously 'for' Elizabeth. She had an open and lively mind and lived in a place and time in which she had to seek out ways to keep that mind active, principally through correspondence with others.

Today we have no shortage of stimulation available, but it's easy to get stuck in a rut. Next time you're looking for a book, show, or podcast, broaden your horizons and pick up something that you wouldn't normally try.

"On a certain night between the conception and birth of the venerable man, an angel of the Lord appeared to his mother in dreams."

ADAMNÁN OF IONA
VITAE COLUMBA/LIFE OF ST COLUMBA
C. 697

EITHNE
HOLY WOMAN

Legend tells that a young woman of the royal family of Ulster was expecting her first baby in the winter of the year 521, when an angel appeared to the woman in a dream. The angel held in his hands the finest cloth she had ever seen, but before she could touch it, it rose up and stretched out in the sky. It floated higher and higher and stretched wider and wider, until it appeared to cover all the territory of Ireland. And still it grew wider, until it covered all the sea and the land beyond. The angel told the amazed young woman that she would give birth to a son who would be a prince and a prophet, and whose message would spread far from his home.

The woman's name was Eithne, and when her child was born, she and her husband entrusted his upbringing to a priest called Cruithneachán. In line with the tradition of the time, Cruithneachán would be his foster father, and train him in wisdom and holiness to ensure he would be fit for the life the prophecy foretold. Cruithneachán was evidently good with children; he is supposed to have taught the child to read using bread letters, like an early version of Alphabetti Spaghetti.

The child would become a prince-monk, and would take the name Colm Cille – Dove of the Church. In English he is known as St Columba. We are told that he founded a monastery at Derry, but left Ireland as penance after a dispute with another holy man ended in bloodshed. Around AD 563 he travelled with twelve companions across the Irish Sea to Scotland. He would go on to found an abbey at Iona and sow the seeds that saw Celtic Christianity become the predominant faith of the country.

Eithne, tradition says, chose to follow her son to Scotland. If this is true, then she was made of stern stuff. Columba and his followers crossed the water in coracles – small, lightweight boats made of willow frames covered in animal hides, designed for ease of movement as each traveller could carry a boat for overland portions of a journey on his or her back. If Eithne travelled with Columba, she would have made part or all of her journeys in this way. And, while not all Irish religious communities of the era were as strict as the modern mind might imagine, the Scottish establishments would not have been luxurious. Commonly the brothers or sisters lived in small cells of stone or wattle (woven wooden strips), and would have been largely self-sufficient, meaning that there was agricultural labour to be done, cloth to weave and so on.

Columba and his contemporaries' establishments were learned places and study and reflection were key. Some sought isolation and travelled to remote places to find it. St Columba is said by his biographer Adamnán to have established a retreat on an island called 'Hinba', and his mother is supposed to have retired there from Iona to live out the rest of her life. The location of 'Hinba' is not confirmed but many believe it to have been Eileach an Naoimh in the archipelago of the Garvellachs in the Firth of Lorne. St Brendan of Clontarf had established a monastery there in the 540s. Today a number of early structures still stand on the islet. One of these is a grave enclosure positioned on a hill, with a slab incised with an equal-armed cross. This is traditionally said to be the grave of Eithne.

We cannot say for sure how much of the tradition pertaining to Eithne is true; fifteen hundred years have passed since Columba was born, and there is no written evidence from her own time for her life. The strong traditions pertaining to her do, however, give an interesting glimpse into female prophecy, women's role in faith communities in early Ireland and Scotland, and the tenacity so many women had then and still have now, in journeying with their families beyond all they know.

LIVE YOUR LIFE BY EITHNE

Eithne, tradition tells us, ended her life in an isolated place of retreat. In today's digitally driven world, it can be hard to find time to be alone with your thoughts. Try to find time every day to step away from your devices and enjoy living in the moment. You might like to try formal mindfulness meditation – many books, apps, classes and other resources exist – or you might simply wish to choose small actions that give you pleasure and focus on those. Eat a ripe apple and take time to enjoy the flavours and sensations. Or breathe in the smell of a brand new book. The idea is to pause and appreciate life a little bit more.

"She had poured out the cocks' blood, cut the animals into pieces and mixed the intestines with spiders and other black worms like scorpions, with a herb called milfoil as well as with other herbs and horrible worms. She had boiled this mixture in a pot with the brains and clothes of a boy who had died without baptism and with the head of a robber who had been decapitated."

PETRONILLA DE MEATH'S 'CONFESSION' OF 1324
AS REPORTED BY THE BISHOP OF OSSUARY

PETRONILLA
DE MEATH
CONDEMNED HERETIC

R ather than 'badass', Petronilla de Meath first went down in history as just 'bad'. From a modern perspective she might be said to have been in the wrong place at the wrong time, belonging to the wrong social class and certainly keeping company with the wrong person. She would pay for it with her life.

Petronilla was born in Meath around the turn of the fourteenth century. By the 1320s she had gone to work as a maid in Kilkenny, in the house of Dame Alice Kyteler, the descendant of successful Flemish merchants. Dame Alice was not entirely popular in the town; she was a very wealthy woman who dabbled in money-lending and in her five decades had got through four husbands. Back in 1302, when Petronilla was still toddling around her parents' home, Dame Alice and her second husband Adam Blund had been accused of the murder of husband number one, William Outlaw, although nothing came of the case.

The spectre of this accusation reared its head again in 1324 when Dame Alice was widowed for the last time, upon the death of John le Poer. Le Poer lingered at the end, during which time he expressed the belief that he had been poisoned. After his death, his offspring teamed up with the children of Alice's previous husbands to accuse her of 'maleficarum', by which means she was supposed to have controlled, murdered or otherwise harmed her poor, late, Christian husbands and amassed her unnatural wealth. She and her associates were supposed to have denied the faith of Christ and the Church, held black magic meetings in churches by night, and chopped up animals as sacrifices to demons by crossroads. Alice herself was accused of possessing a familiar called Robin Artison, who was a demon of Satan. Oh, and the kids were also put out that she showed favouritism to her eldest son, William Outlaw the younger.

As is often the case in accusations of witchcraft against powerful or wealthy women, the accusers had personal axes to grind. In addition to the supposed preference for Wiliam, there was already bad blood on at least one other count. Upon the death of her third husband, Richard Valle, Dame Alice had taken legal action against his son Richard, to force him to pay her widow's dower. Doing your stepmother out of her entitlement on the death of your father isn't a great look, but it pales into insignificance against accusing her – and her friends and servants – of a range of capital crimes.

Dame Alice didn't give in without a fight. She had friends in high places – her money-lending had perhaps helped cement these ties – and she immediately called on their support. The case against her was enthusiastically taken up by Richard de Ledrede, Bishop of Ossuary, who was keen to take on witchcraft more generally. The Bishop was promptly imprisoned by Sir Arnold le Poer, Seneschal of Kilkenny. Undaunted, de Ledrede continued his pursuit of Dame Alice on his release, writing to the Chancellor of Ireland, Roger Utlagh, to demand her arrest. He argued that the secular powers of Ireland should concede to the Church in the case; the charges of heresy were key, since Ireland did not have any formal law on witchcraft at the time. Utlagh was not inclined to help the Bishop since he was related to Alice (his surname is an alternative spelling of 'Outlaw', her first husband's people). Utlagh insisted Alice could not be arrested until she had been excommunicated for forty days. This brought her enough breathing space to flee into his protection.

Things were now rather at an impasse, and sadly this was the point that Petronilla came back into play. Having been accused with Alice, she was tortured and confessed to six of the seven crimes with which they were charged. She also implicated Dame Alice in all.

The Bishop gave an account of her confession, which is filled with just the sort of vivid detail misogynists of the era apparently got off on:

> She said that with her own eyes she had seen the aforesaid demon appear in three, in the form of three black men, each carrying an iron rod in the hand. This apparition happened by daylight before the said Dame Alice, and, while Petronella herself was watching, the apparition had intercourse with Alice. After this disgraceful act, with her own hand she wiped clean the disgusting place with linen from her own bed.

Additionally Petronilla detailed a magical potion she and Alice used on a wooden beam, which allowed them to fly through the sky.

Alice could not have survived the confession, dodgy as it looks to a modern eye, and probably even to non-perverts of the era. She appears to have fled, tradition suggests to England, and there is no further account of her after 1324. Disappointed in the big prize, the Bishop got on with pursuing the poor unfortunates who did not have the means to follow suit.

Petronilla was condemned for 'sorcery, lot taking and offering sacrifices to demons'. The poor woman was flogged 'through six parishes' and burned at the stake on 3 November 1324 in Kilkenny. She was burned for the crime of heresy, but, given that the real object of the trial was the persecution of witches and the use of heresy statute essentially a legal work-around, she is commonly viewed as the first woman in Ireland burned as a witch. She is commemorated as such in a major modern work of feminist art, Judy Chicago's *The Dinner Party*.

LIVE YOUR LIFE BY PETRONILLA

Records pertaining to Petronilla and Alice's case are written from the perspective of those who sought to prosecute them and it is difficult to discern what the relationship may have been between the two women. It was not one of equals, which does not mean it was not one of friendship, but Alice escaped while her employee did not. In fairness to Alice, it might not have been possible to save Petronilla, but on the other hand, neither do we have any evidence to suggest she tried, beyond the tradition that a 'Basil' or 'Basilia' with whom she fled may have been Petronilla's child.

No matter how good your relationship with an employer, you might remember Petronilla and consider how to protect your own rights at work. Make sure you are up-to-speed with company policies and your staff handbook, and join a union. It's always worth having someone else on your side should things go wrong.

MAIRGRÉAG NÍ CHEARBHAILL
MARGARET O'CARROLL
PATRON OF THE ARTS

Margaret O'Carroll of Éile (Ely) in County Offaly was born in the early fifteenth century, and we are lucky enough to have a record of this brilliant woman's activities in the Annals of Connacht and the Annals of the Four Masters. 'Annals' were accounts of the events of a year – think how you might recap your highlights of the past twelve months in a social media post on New Year's Eve – and Ireland's history is preserved in a series of these precious books.

If Margaret were around today, chances are she'd be one of those people whose social media posts are guaranteed to make you feel like a serious underachiever. She was the ultimate hostess, using her position in society to promote her political and cultural interests. Hers was a time of war and conquest and her contribution was in the form of literature and music festivals designed to promote Gaelic culture as a means to resist Norman occupiers.

Modern-day arts festivals are a big deal, involving military-style construction and logistics to bring theatre, book events, music or exhibitions to hundreds or thousands of audience members. Margaret's were no less of an undertaking. She set up two huge extravaganzas in the 1430s with her crack events management team (OK, they weren't called that but she was a queen and had an appropriate retinue at her service). The names of 2,700 attendees were recorded in a roll by a judge called Giolla na Naomh Mac Aodhagáin. These guests were chieftains and poets, musicians, genealogists and other members of the learned and privileged classes. It is likely, based on existing descriptions

"A general invitation was
issued by Mairgreg daughter
of O Cerbaill about the feast
of Dasinchell this year at
Killeigh, and [another] about
the first festival of Mary in the
autumn at Rathangan for the
people who were not with
her at Killeigh, so that she
satisfied fully all the suppliants
of Ireland."

THE ANNALS OF CONNACHT RECORD
MARGARET O'CARROLL'S FESTIVALS
1433

of previous events, that Margaret built a temporary town to house these guests. As a modern-day comparator, the building of the Olympic Village for London 2012 cost in the region of £500 million to house 24,000 athletes. So that would be £50 million for 2,400. We can probably assume that Margaret's labour costs and materials were cheaper, but still it was a phenomenal undertaking indicative of enormous wealth.

Margaret's extravagance extended to her own wardrobe. The chronicler Dubhaltach Mac Fhirbhisigh described her as 'clad in cloath of gold'. She sounds fierce.

Margaret's festivals were of national importance, and her next appearance in the Annals underlines this. This time, in 1445, she appears in the role of negotiator with the English. Her husband Calbhach Ó Conchobhair Failghe had made 'Greate warr' with a family called Bermingham. There was a stalemate; both sides were holding hostages. Without her husband's knowledge, Margaret exchanged the English hostages for the Irish. This was a risky enterprise and indicative of some significant sang-froid on Margaret's part.

In the same year, Margaret joined a party of chiefs and noblewomen on a pilgrimage to Santiago de Compostello in Spain. Again this was no small undertaking; some of her fellow travellers lost their lives on the long, dangerous journey. Margaret made the pilgrimage safely and returned home.

Margaret's other actions challenged the boundaries normally faced by her sex, as Dubhaltach Mac Fhirbhisigh noted in her obituary, writing, 'She was the only woman that has made most of preparing highways, and erecting bridges, churches, and mass-books, and of all manner of things profitable to serve God and her soul.'

Margaret died in 1451, and would be remembered as Mairgréag an Einigh, or 'Margaret the Hospitable'.

LIVE YOUR LIFE BY MARGARET

Margaret died of breast cancer.
Check your boobs, ladies.

GRÁINNE NÍ MHÁILLE
GRACE O'MALLEY
SEA CAPTAIN AND LEADER

Gráinne Ní Mháille has gone down in Irish history as perhaps the ultimate badass. She was born around 1530, into a Gaelic Ireland still largely operating free from English influence. Henry VIII of England styled himself 'Lord of Ireland', but during his reign the native lords and princes took little notice. Gráinne was born into the ruling family of the Ó Máille (O'Malley) dynasty. Her father was Eoghan Dubhdara Ó Máille, who controlled the lands along Clew Bay in County Mayo. The Uí Máille were a seafaring power, with a chain of castles facing the sea. From this base they sailed forth to tax all entering their waters, plunder those who did not comply, and trade or fight as they saw fit. They deferred nominally to their De Búrca (Bourke) overlords, but they were effectively the power in the area. Some hundred years before, they had endowed an Augustinian abbey at Murrisk, indicating vast wealth.

Gráinne's mother was Mairéad (Margaret) or Maedhbh (Maeve), also of the Ó Máille family. Perhaps it was for this dual ancestry that Gráinne became her father's heir, despite the fact that Eoghan had a son from another relationship, Dónall na Píoba ('Donald of the Pipes').

In 1546 Gráinne married the fearsomely named Dónall an Chogaidh ('Donald of Warfare'), *tánaiste* or heir to the chief of the Ó Flaithbheartaigh (O'Flaherty), whose territories lay in modern-day Connemara. The marriage produced three children: Eoghan, Méadhbh and Murchadh. In 1565, Dónall an Chogaidh was killed in an ambush by political rivals. Gráinne left her husband's

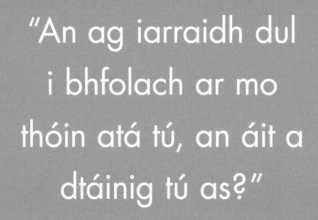

"An ag iarraidh dul
i bhfolach ar mo
thóin atá tú, an áit a
dtáinig tú as?"

"Do you want to hide in my arse,
the place you came out of?"

GRÁINNE NÍ MHÁILLE CHIDES HER SON
FOR SHIRKING HIS DUTY IN BATTLE
IN AN ACECDOTE FROM ORAL TRADITION

family lands and returned home to her own, where she set up her principal residence on Clare Island. Tradition has it that she consoled herself by taking a lover, but the relationship ended in bloodshed when he was killed by a rival family. Gráinne is said to have killed the murderers herself in vengeance, and engaged in ongoing aggression against the family to which they belonged.

Whether or not the story of the affair is true, we know that Gráinne married again, around 1566, to Ridseard an Iarainn ('Iron Richard') de Búrca, whose nickname derived from the ironworks on his land. From this marriage was born Teabóid na Long ('Tibbot of the Ships'), reportedly delivered at sea as Gráinne prepared to attack Barbary pirates. He did not, apparently, inherit his mother's feisty, fiery and fierce spirit, and her traditional rebuke to him for cowardice can be seen opposite.

During Gráinne's lifetime, English control of Ireland increased significantly. In 1576, Gráinne took part in the 'surrender and regrant' process for her lands with Tudor Lord Deputy Sir Henry Sidney. Under this system, she gave up her hereditary Gaelic right to the lands and then received them back under the English ownership system, with various conditions of loyalty. Gráinne may have done this relatively cynically; her lands were days' march from Dublin and she spent much of her time at sea, making the chance of Crown control fairly slight. Sidney seemed to take her compliance at face value, reporting later, 'there came to mee a most famous femynyne sea captain called Grace Imallye, and offred her service unto me, wheresoever I woulde command her, with three gallyes and two hundred fightinge men . . .' Despite these words, however, Gráinne did little or nothing to support the English forces, and plenty to obstruct them. There were multiple retaliatory actions, such as an attack on her castle on Clare Island in 1579, an arrest in 1586, and the arrest of her sons Teabóid and Murchadh and her half-brother Dónall in 1593. These last two were actions of Sir Richard Bingham, governor of Connacht, who considered Gráinne to be 'nurse to all rebellions in the province for this forty years'. Bingham also seized her ships and cattle, rendering her – by her own account – near penniless.

In 1593 Gráinne decided to dispatch a petition to Queen Elizabeth I of England, with a plea for help. Elizabeth sent Gráinne a list of questions in return. Gráinne answered these with some skill, detailing how she had been 'constrayned . . . to take arms and by force to maintaine her selfe and her people by sea and land', given Bingham's callous cruelty. She described his chilling treatment of her when he had her arrested in 1586. Bingham, she wrote, 'caused a new pair of gallows to be made for her last funerall wher shy thought to end her daies'. Gráinne's answers were reviewed by the queen's secretary Sir Walter Burghley, and despite his advice, Elizabeth agreed to meet with Gráinne at Greenwich Palace.

At the meeting, both women were arrayed in their best, and surrounding by courtiers and Elizabeth's royal guards. One story maintains that Gráinne also had a knife about her person, but this was discovered and removed before the meeting, with the explanation accepted that she carried it only to ensure her own safety. Gráinne, it is said, refused to bow to Elizabeth, as she did not recognise the Tudor queen as her sovereign, but rather as an equal since Gráinne regarded herself also a queen. She then continued – the story goes – to exhibit her own brand of personal style by accepting a lace handkerchief from a lady of the court to stifle a sneeze and then throwing the fine item on the fire.

Gráinne was not a native English speaker and Elizabeth spoke no Irish; traditionally it is said that the meeting, therefore, was carried out in Latin. The two women reached a rapprochement; Elizabeth agreed to remove Richard Bingham from his position in Ireland and to return various property to Gráinne, and Gráinne agreed to stop supporting the Irish lords in their actions against the English crown. Indeed, Elizabeth did remove Bingham, but Gráinne's property was never returned and, eventually, Bingham made his way back to Ireland. Gráinne concluded that the meeting had achieved nothing, and reinstated her support for the Irish lords in the Nine Years' War. Initially this saw some Irish success, but the Irish lords were defeated at Kinsale in 1602, and Gaelic power in Ireland was broken.

Gráinne died around 1603. Even after her death her fame lived on as 'a notorious woman in all the coasts of Ireland' and as a heroine of Gaelic resistance to Tudor rule. Much of her story, however, is lost to us. Gaelic aristocratic families of her era kept great books that recorded their genealogies, histories and literature. Gráinne's story might have been recorded in the book of the Ó Máille, but it has been lost or destroyed. The main written sources we have for Gráinne's life are in English, including Elizabeth's questions and Gráinne's answers, held today in the National Archives in London. Oral tradition in Ireland also kept her memory alive, and perhaps in the way that is truest to the spirit of this remarkable woman.

LIVE YOUR LIFE BY GRÁINNE

Gráinne got her meeting with Elizabeth through a bit of clever writing, in the form of her answers to Elizabeth's 'interrogatories'. You can power-up your own writing too. Unless you're actually writing about feelings (e.g. in a love letter or a sympathy card), avoid writing about how you 'feel'. If you write 'I felt that this was unfair,' it's quite easy for someone else to avoid answering your point by saying, 'I'm sorry you felt that way', as though the problem is your emotions as opposed to the thing that happened. Try verbs like 'consider' instead. 'I considered this was unfair for the following reasons . . .' is more likely to get you what you want, whether that's an apology, compensation, a change in policy or whatever.

A NOTE ON GRÁINNE'S NAME

Gráinne is known by many names, which aim to anglicise either her given name and kindred (Grace O'Malley has stuck, but documents from her time spell Gráinne as Grany, Granny, Grayn or Granee). She was also known as Gráinne Mhaol, literally 'bare/bald Gráinne', and this has been borrowed into English as *Granuaile*. The story goes that her father refused to take her on an expedition owing to the fact she was a girl; Gráinne immediately cut off her hair to appear as a boy. This may be a folk etymology – a false explanation attached to a name – and it may truly derive from family territory at Umhalls.

"Mary, I pray the(e), let the(e) and I be friends for I beare thee noe ill will, and I pray the(e), doe thou beare me none."

FLORENCE NEWTON 'CURSES' MARY LONGDON
WITH KIND WORDS
1660, FROM TESTIMONY OF 1661

FLORENCE NEWTON

'WITCH'

When Petronilla de Meath died for her part in her mistress Alice Kyteler's supposed sorcery (see page 95), Ireland had no witchcraft legislation. Instead, Petronilla was burned for heresy. By the time Florence Newton of Youghal in Cork was accused three hundred years later, the Tudors had generously bestowed upon Ireland all the legal frameworks and associated obscenity necessary to carry out the torture and judicial murder of elderly, infirm and otherwise vulnerable women.

Florence wasn't very badass; rather, she was 'old and disquieted, and distracted with her own suffering', which made her a perfect candidate for a bit of persecution. It seems likely that she was also hungry, since she approached John Pyne's housemaid Mary Longdon to beg for a piece of salt beef in the winter of 1660. It was Christmas-time, after all, when goodwill to all men is all the rage; Florence might even have hoped for something warm to drink. The Bible says that Mary found shelter in the stable; her namesake in Youghal sent an old woman off into the cold to starve.

Perhaps Florence was a better Christian than Mary Longdon; she apparently determined to make amends for any offence she had caused. Mary was out and about with her washing pail when Florence surprised her, planted a kiss on her and said she hoped they could be friends. Mary soon began to suffer from all sorts of odd ailments, from violent fits to vomiting up needles, pins, straw and other household items. She exhibited unusual strength and was hit by mysterious stones flung by an unseen hand, saw visions and apparently floated up to the ceiling. In her visions she identified Florence Newton, inviting Mary to become a witch. Mary's symptoms miraculously improved when Florence was locked in irons.

Mary Longdon initially implicated two other women as well as Florence but took this testimony back when the Mayor of Youghal threatened all three with a test by water. This would involve being thrown off a boat with opposite thumbs and big toes tied together. The idea was that water would reject the impure body of a witch, she would float and could be fished out for trial. If she was 'innocent', well . . . *damned if you do, damned if you don't* is the saying that comes to mind.

Florence was then jailed and 'tested' while she awaited trial, by being cut on the arms with a lance and stabbed with an awl in the hand. She was also subject to some odd processes aimed at using a sort of counter-magic to catch her out (presumably this was the 'good' kind of magic practised by good people and so allowed). On one occasion her testers stabbed a stool while she sat on it, and on another Mary Langdon's urine was dropped onto a red-hot tile from the prison building, which supposedly caused Florence some ill-effects.

For her supposed crimes against Mary, Florence would not have faced execution, but rather imprisonment. While she was in prison, however, matters took a turn for the worse. Among Florence's failings was an inability to say the Lord's Prayer. A jailer tried to help her; Florence kissed his hand through the bars. The man became convinced he was cursed and died a couple of weeks later. A 'kiss of death' narrative then emerged; Florence was also retrospectively accused of having killed a number of children by kissing them.

Florence stood trial at Cork Assizes on 11 September 1661. A manuscript source for the trial reads, 'Florence Newton of yoghall spinster dyed aboute sixty five or there abouts att the last Assizes held for the County of Corke the Eleventh of September 1661.' This could mean that Florence was executed, but without reference to a verdict or means of execution (it would have been hanging for killing by witchcraft), it is possible that she died during the trial. It would scarcely have been of 'natural causes' given all that had been done to her, but at least she may not have suffered the rope.

Florence died shortly after the Restoration of Charles II, when many Protestants in Ireland were feeling particularly insecure. Most had supported Oliver Cromwell's regime; now there was a new Stuart monarch on the throne.

Clusters of witch persecutions are often associated with political instability of this type. The whole community of Youghal certainly seemed to get involved in Florence's case, from observing Mary's convulsions to testifying – often second-hand – against the 'witch'.

The motivations of the individual players is hard to discern at this distance. Mary Longdon's contribution as a 'demoniac' is not unique; the Salem trials, for example, were also based on young women exhibiting similar 'symptoms'. Given the circumscribed lives of girls at the time, many have speculated that there was a perverse power in causing trouble for their elders, and of course their behaviour earned them significant attention. As for Florence, why she was so keen on kissing people she'd fallen out with is not clear. It might have been a genuine gesture of conciliation after giving offence. It could have been intended to antagonise. It could indicate an isolated woman, possibly suffering from dementia, making a child-like gesture, or an erotically charged one. It does have echoes in witch narratives elsewhere, for example in a Scottish ballad, 'Alison Cross', in which a man resists a witch's overtures, specifically her kiss.

Ireland held very few witchcraft trials by comparison with Scotland, and those it did hold were generally in 'planted' Protestant communities. Gaelic Ireland seems to have had little interest in persecuting witches. Perhaps women held more power, or perhaps cultural traditions saw magic as relatively benign, even an everyday occurrence. Since 80 per cent of Ireland's population belonged to this group, its women were safer than their sisters elsewhere from at least one of the evils of the age.

LIVE YOUR LIFE BY FLORENCE

The behaviour of accusers in witch panics found a modern echo in the early days of the 2020 Covid-19 epidemic, when people across the UK and Ireland developed a particular interest in monitoring the behaviour of others. At its height this took the form of shaming individuals on social media and reporting neighbours to the police for infringement of social distancing and other laws. There is little evidence to suggest that finger-pointing is ever a productive way to influence others and it's not good for you, either. Remember Florence's sad experiences and try to find ways to be a positive member of your community, on and offline.

CHRISTIAN DAVIES

SOLDIER

The Battle of Landen in 1693 was not a good day for France's enemies in the Nine Years' War; in fact, it was a pretty bad day for the French as well. Their commander managed to trap the Allied forces in a dangerous position, and then achieved victory through sheer weight of numbers, but there were heavy losses to both sides. British soldier Christopher Welch was wounded in the fighting and captured by the French. Welch fought as an infrantryman in Captain Tichborne's company of foot, and was not returned to the British Army until the following year, when a prisoner exchange made it possible.

Welch returned to standard duties in the company but things went wrong soon after. A dispute over a woman escalated into a duel; in this fight, Welch killed a sergeant of the company and was discharged from the British Army. Two re-enlistments followed with the 4th Dragoons – later called the 2nd Royal North British Dragoons and more commonly known as the 'Scots Greys'. Welch again fought in the Nine Years' War, and later in the War of the Spanish Succession.

Welch's life was not without scandal. In addition to the duel, a prostitute claimed that Welch had fathered her child; Welch did not deny this and an agreement was reached regarding financial support. Welch's ability to meet these payments may have been boosted by an apparent enthusiasm for looting and marauding in the aftermath of battle.

In 1704 Welch received a musket ball in the leg at the Battle of Schellenberg, but fought on with the ball still in situ through the Battle of Blenheim. Blenheim

"I observed a
woman, with
a visible Joy in
her face, make up
to a man, whom,
by his side face,
I fancied I had
known . . ."

FROM *MOTHER ROSS*
DANIEL DEFOE
1744

was a decisive Allied victory, and Welch was assigned to guard French prisoners in the aftermath. This brought Welch into contact with the 1st Regiment of Foot, where one private was apparently consorting with a Dutch woman and incurred Welch's wrath for it. This was perhaps not surprising; Welch was, in fact, married to the private. Welch, you see, was a woman in disguise.

'Welch' was born Christian Cavanagh in Dublin in 1667 and was known as Kit. It would come in handy that this is also a nickname for Christopher when Kit's husband Richard Welsh disappeared. (His name was variously also written Welch or Walsh; they weren't hung up on spelling in the 1600s.) It subsequently transpired that Welsh had ended up in the British Army. At the time Kit was the mother of two small children with a third on the way, and running a pub in Dublin. She delivered her youngest child, bundled all three off to her mother, cropped her hair and headed off to track Richard down. Now 'Kit' was short for 'Christopher', and somehow the fact that 'Welch' was a woman passed unnoticed in the army despite the close quarters in which soldiers slept, ate, dressed and urinated. Kit used a contraption involving a silver tube to manage the latter issue, like some kind of seventeenth-century Shewee.

Having found her husband in a compromising situation, Kit was unimpressed, but relations thawed to the degree that the pair agreed to maintain the 'Christopher Welch' charade by pretending to be brothers. They pulled it off until 1706, when Kit suffered a wound to the head and was seen by an army surgeon. The secret was out, but the regiment stood by 'Mrs Welsh', paying her until she recovered and subsequently allowing her to transfer to her husband's regiment as an army wife and provisioner. Her fiery spirit continued; she is said to have attacked a mistress of her husband's and cut off her nose.

Richard Welsh died in the bloodbath of the Battle of Malplaquet in 1709. Kit subsequently took up with a Captain Ross in her old regiment – she added 'Mother Ross' to her already impressive list of aliases – and then one Hugh Jones, a dragoon. She married Jones, but he died in 1710.

Kit came back to Britain with her regiment in 1712, and was presented to Queen Anne. She returned home and married a fellow Dubliner in 1713 – Davies was the last name she added to her arsenal. The couple lived an itinerant lifestyle in Ireland and England until, in old age, Kit became a Chelsea Pensioner. She was buried there with military honours in 1739.

Kit's incredible story was told – in varying degrees of probability – in a book anonymously published in 1744 under the catchy title *Mother Ross: The Life and Adventures of Christian Davies, commonly called Mother Ross, on Campaign with the Duke of Marlborough*. The book is commonly considered to be the work of Daniel Defoe and has generally been published under his name. As a result, Kit is perhaps the best known of a number of fierce and fiery women who fought in the British Army in her era.

LIVE YOUR LIFE BY CHRISTIAN

You've got to give it to Kit – she was determined. Whatever your goals are, take a leaf out of her book and go for it. If it helps to hold yourself to account, get yourself a notebook, plan the steps you need to take and keep a diary of your progress. The key thing is to make your objectives SMART – specific, measurable, achievable, results-focused and time-scaled. This is common business jargon but don't let that put you off – it's common because it really does work.

ANNE BONNY

PIRATE

n common with many women born in Ireland in the last three hundred years, Anne Bonny's story is one of emigration. Otherwise, her life was quite remarkable, since her trade was piracy. You don't get much more 'badass' than that.

Anne was born around the year 1700, and grew up first in her native Ireland, then in London and latterly in Carolina. Although verifiable sources for her life are scarce, tradition has it that she was born in Cork, in Old Head of Kinsale, to Mary Brennan, a servant, and Mary's employer, William McCormac. They needed #MeToo back then as much as we need it now.

William McCormac was a lawyer, and he is reported to have fled to London with his illegitimate daughter. There Anne was routinely dressed as a boy and McCormac began to train her as a lawyer's clerk. Eventually this irregular family unit emigrated to Carolina, where William McCormac found it prudent to drop 'Mc' from his name and instead become plain old 'Cormac'. Eventually he prospered.

The Cormac/Brennan household was not a particularly happy one, and when Anne was in her late teens she risked her father's disapproval to marry a sailor and small-time pirate named James Bonny. Anne and Bonny moved to Nassau in New Providence in the Bahamas, where they could find sanctuary in the so-called 'Republic of Pirates'. James Bonny quickly established himself there as an informant to the Crown.

Piracy was a popular occupation across the Caribbean in Anne's time, as the end of the War of the Spanish Succession had left a large number of sailors

"[they] wore men's jackets, and long trousers, and handkerchiefs tied about their heads: and . . . each of them had a machete and pistol in their hands and they cursed and swore at the men to murder her"

DOROTHY THOMAS'S IMPRESSION OF
ANNE BONNY AND MARY READ
1720

and privateers without other means of earning a wage. Living in this milieu seems to have suited Anne, and she took up with one John Rackham, an English pirate known as 'Calico Jack'. Rackham had become captain of an infamous pirate ship, the *Ranger*, and had operated relatively successfully for a time despite various encounters with the authorities. When he met Anne, he was enjoying a brief time ashore as a supposedly law-abiding citizen, having sought a pardon from Woodes Rodger, Governor of the Bahamas. Supposedly Anne herself was the undoing of Calico Jack's good intentions: Anne's husband accused her of adultery as the relationship between the two developed, she was sentenced to a public whipping, Calico Jack offered to buy her out of her marriage and, when her husband refused, the two stole a sloop and put to sea. Governor Rodger issued a proclamation declaring Calico Jack and crew pirates.

Piracy was clearly not a particularly ethical profession, but interestingly Calico Jack had an eye to equal opportunities – his crew included not only Anne but also Mary Read, an Englishwoman. Mary seems to have been introduced to dressing as a male by her own mother in order to claim a false inheritance. Read had even had a stint in the British Army, and tradition has it that neither Anne nor Calico Jack realised she was a woman when she first joined them. Or possibly they did; her disguise was not sufficient to fool a female victim, Dorothy Thomas, who clocked both Anne and Mary as women owing to their breasts.

Before justice caught up with Calico Jack and crew, Anne spent some time ashore in Cuba, where she gave birth to a child. She was pregnant again when the crew was captured after a bout of heavy drinking in October 1720, as was Mary Read. Calico Jack was tried and sentenced to death; he was hanged at Port Royal in Jamaica on 18 November 1720, and his body displayed on an island near the entrance to Port Royal Harbour. The women 'pleaded their bellies', i.e. stated that they were pregnant and therefore could not be executed. Mary Read died in prison of a fever in 1721; it seems likely that this was puerperal fever as a result of giving birth in squalid conditions. No official record exists of the fate of Anne Bonny or her child, although her story concludes as follows in Charles Johnson's book *A General History of the Robberies and Murders of the most notorious Pyrates* in 1724: 'She was continued in Prison, to the Time of her lying in, and afterwards reprieved from Time to Time; but what is become of her since, we cannot tell; only this we know, that she was not executed.'

LIVE YOUR LIFE BY ANNE

Being a 'Notorious Pyrate' is not a great job for grown-ups, but small people like a bit of dress-up now and then. In today's world children's toys, books and clothes are depressingly gendered, and kit that promotes more rambunctious play is too often geared exclusively towards boys. For the little people in your life, seek out equality in play. Search for #LetToysBeToys to find out more.

PEG WOFFINGTON

ACTRESS

Margaret Woffington – known as Peg – was born in Dublin around the mid-years of the 1710s. Her family were not wealthy, and after the death of her father, John, she, her mother Hannah and her sister Polly found themselves in dire straits. Her mother turned to the miserable occupation of taking in laundry to support them, while Peg supplemented the meagre income this secured by selling watercress door-to-door.

Peg was an exceptionally pretty girl, and when she was around ten years old, she caught the eye of one Madame Violante while at market. Madame or Signora Violante was a tightrope-walker, acrobat and *commedia dell'arte* actor. Having wowed London and Bristol – where her husband Signor Violante had crossed the River Severn by tightrope – she had set up in Dublin, where she established the Dame Street Booth. Madame sought Peg's mother's permission to apprentice her daughter to the company, which she evidently secured since Peg began to appear in what Violante termed their 'Liliputian' productions – we might call these 'youth theatre' today. She was a particular hit as Polly Peachum in *The Beggar's Opera*.

Peg worked for a time in Dublin, appearing on the bill at the Theatre Royal, the Smock Alley Theatre and elsewhere. The links between the London and Dublin theatre scenes in the eighteenth century were incredibly strong – considering the perilous sea-crossing between the two – and inevitably Peg caught the eye of the London theatre set. An offer was made by John Rich, manager at Covent

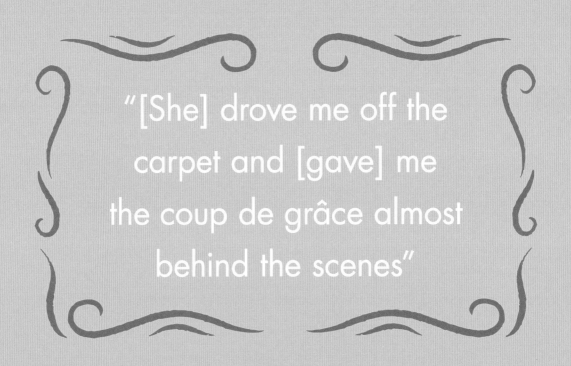

"[She] drove me off the carpet and [gave] me the coup de grâce almost behind the scenes"

GEORGE ANN BELLAMY DESCRIBES HER STABBING BY PEG WOFFINGTON
IN *AN APOLOGY FOR THE LIFE OF GEORGE ANN BELLAMY* VOL I
BY HERSELF
1785

Garden, to perform in his theatre. Her first role there was Sylvia in *The Recruiting Officer*, Irish writer George Farquhar's infamous Restoration comedy.

Like Nell Gwyn before her, light-hearted material was Peg's forte, and she was less popular in tragic roles, although she was not entirely unsuccessful in her forays into Shakespeare. Also like Nell, Peg became well known for her 'breeches roles,' i.e. appearing in male parts. She played Sir Harry Wildair in *The Constant Couple* to some acclaim; the part had been something of a hero role for the actor Robert Wilks and it is rather diverting to think that women had their revenge for the centuries they'd been barred from the stage by taking the plum male roles too. A portrait of Peg by the artist John Lewis, from 1753, shows her in a somewhat masculine-looking hat and rather demonstrates the way in which the fashions of the era might have lent themselves to cross-dressing on the stage. The portrait hangs today in London, in the National Portrait Gallery, and is one of a number in existence of Peg, who was considered quite the society beauty.

Peg was called 'Mrs Margaret Woffington' on playbills although she never married. This has been interpreted variously as an affectation of Peg's, or a slight by her employers. It may simply have been that the prefix was routinely added to mature women's names – a Mrs Nell on a bill of 1664 is probably Nell Gwyn, at the ripe old age of twenty-something. Peg was most definitely not without male company, however – first she lived with actor Charles Macklin, before embarking on an affair with David Garrick, the greatest actor of the day. Her other lovers included an earl and an MP. Her relationships with women were not always so positive. In the competitive world of the London stage, Peg was known for her enmities, and particularly for her loathing of fellow Irish-born actress Catherine 'Kitty' Clive. She also stabbed her countrywoman Mrs George Anne Bellamy during a performance, over a quarrel relating to Mrs Bellamy having turned up in purposely ostentatious Paris gowns two nights in a row.

Peg was a trailblazer in many ways. John Rich, who had scouted her in Dublin all those years before, set up a 'Beefsteak Club', an all-male dining club of a type popular at the time. Rich's club – known as the 'Sublime Society of Steaks' – claimed Garrick as a member, along with many of the great writers and artists of the age, including Samuel Johnson and William Hogarth. Peg was not, of course, eligible to join, but join she did, and was suitable badass even to be elected president.

Peg and David Garrick's relationship ended in the mid-1740s, apparently because Peg resented the degree to which he wished to control her life and career. She lived a somewhat peripatetic life thereafter, with a house at Teddington in Middlesex and sojourns in Paris, London and Dublin. She amassed a little wealth by way of a bequest from a fellow Irish actor – for which purpose it appears she converted to Protestantism – but continued to appear on the stage, where she could command high fees.

Peg never took her final curtain call; while playing Rosalind in *As You Like It* in 1757, she collapsed on stage in paralysis. Her acting career was over and she was bed-ridden for most of the remainder of her days. She died in 1760, in her forties, and was buried at Teddington. Her memorial stone gives 1720 as her date of birth but this is probably not correct.

Despite her 'queenly' manners around other actresses, Peg did not forget her humble beginnings. She supported both her mother and her sister Polly financially, and in her will she provided for the building of almshouses at Teddington. Sister Polly inherited the balance of her fortune.

Peg was not forgotten after her death. A eulogy was written by dramatist Henry Jones and she appeared in Charles Lee Lewes' *Memoir* in 1805. In 1852 the dramatist and author Charles Reade based his play *Masks and Faces* on her life, and, after it became a hit, produced the novelisation *Peg Woffington* the following year. These accounts, however, focused more on her relationships than her career, doing a disservice to one of the greatest actresses of her generation.

LIVE YOUR LIFE BY PEG

Many women today continue to struggle owing to male-only clubs. It's legal for clubs to exist that are uniquely for a membership with a protected characteristic – so a rugby club might exist that is only for women and not men, or a club for people who are deaf – but the concern many have regarding men's clubs specifically is that often these are a place where business or political connections are forged, and women are not invited in. This is not OK. Before you give your vote to a political party, seek reassurance that memberships of candidates within your preferred political party are properly registered, and call out anything that is of concern.

"The antiquated Maidens, frequenters of the Tea and Card-tables, hinted they might take a peep in private, for they were sure my Book must offer some nice tit bits, and delicious morsels of scandal."

MEMOIRS OF MRS. MARGARET LEESON VOL. 1
WRITTEN BY HERSELF
1795

PEG PLUNKETT
AKA MARGARET LEESON
COURTESAN

n contrast with the life of Nell Gwyn (see page 169), which is preserved almost entirely in the writings of others, Dublin's fiercest and most infamous courtesan derived great pleasure from the telling of her own story. In this way she took control of her own legend, and made a pretty penny in the process.

By her own account, Margaret Plunkett – known informally as Peg – was born into some comfort in Killough in Westmeath, where her father had property and her mother connections. She was one of an eye-watering twenty-two children, of whom only eight lived beyond infancy. The surviving children received a good education – an assertion proven in Peg's case by the quality of her writing – and the elder made good marriages. But disaster struck in the form of smallpox, killing Peg's mother and eldest brother, devastating her father and placing the family under the less-than-tender mercies of the next eldest boy, Christopher. Peg describes Christopher as a near-demon, who resented his siblings' claims on the family fortune and attempted to deprive them of it by any means possible. When he refused his consent to Margaret's older sister to make a good marriage in hopes of depriving her of her marriage portion, said sister relinquished all claim on the money, married the lad anyway, and carried young Peg off with them to Dublin.

In the city, Peg was in her element. She took full part in the social whirl and soon was drowning in marriage proposals, but the wretched Christopher refused his consent to any and all of these. Instead he carted Peg home and renewed his tyranny; she escaped as and when she could but the abuse continued whenever she was at home. Eventually she left for Dublin for good where, exhausted and depressed, she was easy prey for one Mr Dardis, an acquaintance of her brother-in-law. Peg took her share of the blame ('How can I call him seducer, when I met the seduction halfway?'), but the modern reader can't help but note that she was a child by the standards of today. Soon she was in the family way and Mr Dardis was prevailed upon to maintain her outside the city. The arrangement ended when the child died.

Thrown off by her relations – who had discovered the whole circumstance despite Peg's attempts to hush it up – she briefly became the mistress of a wine merchant, and then of an English 'Mr Leeson', whose name she would use on and off for the rest of her life. He may have been Joseph Leeson, 2nd Earl of Millport. He was definitely one for double standards; while he had Peg as his bit on the side, he was unimpressed when he discovered that she, too, had other liaisons, and he ended the affair. For her part, Peg said that she, 'at that time, was fully persuaded that Polygamy was not wrong in its own nature'.

Peg then turned her attentions back to her other admirers, spending five years with a Mr Lawless, to whom she bore five children. He too was a very jealous lover, and latterly came to suspect Peg of infidelity. As their relationship deteriorated, so too did their finances, and none of their children survived infancy. Eventually Lawless abandoned Peg, leaving her a note before sailing to America. She was pregnant at the time, and did not expect to carry the child to term, but a daughter arrived safely.

Peg credited Lawless's desertion of her with turning her into a 'coquet', and when some time had passed – and another daughter arrived – she determined to set up in business as an 'impure'. She and her friend Sally Hayes took a house on Drogheda Street, which they operated as a brothel staffed by a cast of 'nymphs'. This safe haven was quickly tarnished, however, when it was attacked by a notorious Dublin gang of wealthy louts known as the 'Pinking Dindies', led by one Robert Crosbie. The gang demanded entrance to the house, whereupon they proceeded to smash windows and destroy all in their path. A heavily pregnant Peg was beaten and her young daughter terrorised. Neither the daughter nor the unborn child survived the ordeal. Peg took Crosbie to court, despite his threats that he would shoot her – she retorted that she would have her own pistols to hand. She won her damages, and moved her establishment first to Wood Street, and then on to Pitt Street, where she attracted a wealthy clientele from Dublin's highest social circles.

Peg was a hugely successful madam, in no small part because she was a good sport whose sense of humour and wit combined with a cunning in what we might, today, call 'marketing'. The more she was spoken of, the better known her bawdy house became, and so she appeared at all the best places scandalously attired; once as virgin goddess Diana at a masquerade ball and on another occasion in Dublin's first ever bell-hooped skirt. She fought for her right to take her place in society, taking legal action against an opera impresario who refused her access to his theatre and even insisting on riding side-by-side with royalty when her carriage encountered the Prince Regent's. 'I think part of the road was for my use,' said Peg pertly when her companions protested, 'as well as for that of the king, and if you English are servile and timid, we Irish are not.'

After many years in business, Peg determined to retire. At this juncture, however, she had many debtors, and struggled to extract payment. She hit on the rather ingenious solution of writing her memoirs, which paid in its own right and also may have focused minds on settling monies owing. Volumes I and II were significant hits, packed with racy anecdotes and revelations. Peg, however, did not live to see the memoirs completed with the publication of Volume III; she died in 1797 at the age of seventy. Her obituary appeared in the *Dublin Evening Post*, which rather sweetly reported, 'She figured for a long time in the bon ton – and absolutely made the fashion. It was her practice to confine her favours to a temporary husband. In this state she lived with several gentlemen in the style of fashionable elegance.'

LIVE YOUR LIFE BY PEG

Peg knew her rights – and she enthusiastically pursued them, in the courts if necessary. From consumer rights to employment law, tenants' rights to welfare, you can benefit from knowing a bit about your own. Citizens Information in Ireland and Citizens Advice in the UK are great places to start, with huge amounts of information on all these areas, and more.

"The great wonder was
that the machinery of life
could have been carried on
for so long in so minute and
diminutive a form."

THE LITERARY GAZETTE
REPORTS CAROLINE CRACHAMI'S DEATH
1824

CAROLINE FOGHELL
AKA CAROLINE CRACHAMI
'MARVEL'

n 1824, London's New Bond Street played host to Caroline Crachami, the so-called 'Sicilian Fairy'. She was nine years old and accounts of her height differ, but it was recorded at as little as nineteen and a half inches high. Visitors flocked to see 'the smallest of all persons mentioned in the records of littleness'. If visitors paid an extra shilling, they were permitted to pick her up and 'handle' her.

Caroline was indeed half-Sicilian, and the other half was Irish. Her father, Louis Vogel, was a Sicilian soldier and musician. Her mother, generally described as an Italian lady, is now thought actually to have been Margaret Norton of Mallow in County Cork. This would certainly explain the family's presence in Dublin during Caroline's early years. Her father would later adopt a more Irish-sounding version of his own name, Lewis Foghell or Fogle.

Caroline was one of five children, and the only one with restricted growth. She was a fragile child, able to walk, although unsteady on her feet. She could speak too, but said very little, and nothing of import, in a weak voice. She liked pretty things, clothes, and anything sparkly and it seems she loved music.

The family moved to Dublin when Caroline was a child, and crossed the path of a young doctor who professed an interest in seeing Caroline. His name was Dr Gilligan, and he worked at the Lying-In Hospital, which is known as the Rotunda today. He may have attended Caroline's mother when one of the other children were born. In any case, he met Caroline in 1823, when she was eight.

Gilligan had lived in London during his training, and impressed on the Foghells that Caroline's health would be best served there, where the climate was better than in Ireland. He offered to take Caroline himself, and since the family could not begin to afford such an expense, he sought their permission to exhibit Caroline to the paying public to meet her costs.

It is difficult to discern with any certainty the family's reason for giving up Caroline to Gilligan's care, except to observe that they were poor, and a doctor would have been a trusted and revered figure in their world. For whatever reason, they gave their permission, and Gilligan took the child to Liverpool.

In Liverpool Caroline acquired a new surname – 'Crackham'. Gilligan claimed he was her father, advertised her as coming from Sicily – it was half true – and charged admittance to see her. She was exhibited from early in the morning until late at night, but Gilligan was disappointed in the crowds and decided to move on. He tried Manchester and Birmingham before they finally reached London in spring 1824.

Caroline was by now named Crachami, the better to promote her Sicilian origins, and she attraced a high class of clientele. She was even presented to King George IV, in special robes procured for the occasion. The popularity of the exhibition at New Bond Street soared and some two hundred people a day came to see her. At last Gilligan had his success, but Caroline was now seriously ill with tuberculosis, and in June she died.

Contemporary reports say that Caroline's parents learned of her death via an article in *The Dublin Journal*. In distress that can only be imagined, her father left immediately for London. There he found Gilligan gone. He owed rent and he had apparently taken Caroline's body with him.

After some searching, Gilligan's landlord directed the bereaved father to the surgeon Sir Everhard Home, who had been a patron of Gilligan's and had made the introduction to the king. Home was able to tell Foghell that Gilligan had made an arrangement with the Royal College of Surgeons to sell Caroline's corpse to them. He had subsequently upped his price; the college had not agreed but had accepted the corpse and undertaken to reach a settlement later. Home had delivered her to the dissecting room himself, 'in a box'.

Contemporary accounts describe Caroline's father bursting into the dissection and disrupting the process. He is supposed to have refused to leave until a guarantee was given that no further desecration would take place. If this was ever promised, the promise was not honoured. Caroline's body was fully dissected and her skeleton mounted for display. It is still on show in the Hunterian Museum, with a box of tiny possessions Caroline owned in life.

After much debate in the twentieth century regarding Caroline's age and condition, today she lends her name to a type of osteodysplastic primordial dwarfism (ODPD). Study of her remains has allowed paediatricians to differentiate a group of patients with disease characteristics similar to hers – 'Type Caroline Crachami'.

LIVE YOUR LIFE BY CAROLINE

I t's hard to know where to start in terms of what's wrong in Caroline's story. Parental neglect, callous abuse and exploitation, sentimental appropriation and objectification . . . the list goes on.

Take inspiration from this truly sad story of a child failed by everyone around her, and make sure you do all you can to help the children in your life grow into resilient, happy adults. Resist the temptation to 'baby' children as they grow by doing things for them that they are capable of doing for themselves. Give them time and space to figure it out, and don't crumble the instant they become frustrated – dealing with frustration is an essential skill in life.

"both from the literary and scientific standpoints she must be ranked as a great scientific writer"

AGNES CLERKE'S OBITUARY
THE TIMES
1907

AGNES CLERKE

ASTRONOMER

gnes Clerke was born in Skibereen in County Cork in 1842, one of three children of a bank manager and the daughter of a brewer. Her father John was a classics graduate with a passion for mathematics and astronomy, which he shared with his daughter. John's wife Catherine was also intellectual, with a gift for music, and from her Agnes inherited a lifelong love of the piano. Agnes and her siblings' young years coincided with those of the Irish Famine, which severely affected the area around Skibereen. Perhaps the misery on their doorstep motivated John and Catherine to educate their children at home, in an atmosphere of serious study. Agnes's interest in astronomy was furthered by access to her father's transit telescope, with which he both viewed the planets and offered an accurate local time service by tracking the transit of stars. At the age of just fifteen Agnes had begun work on a history of astronomy.

When Agnes was nineteen, the family left Skibereen for Dublin, where her brother Aubrey entered university. Hers was an era in which warm climates were considered beneficial for the health, and this lay behind a further move to Italy in 1867. Agnes and her sister Ellen lived in Florence for a decade, pursuing various courses of study and becoming fluent in a number of languages.

Agnes's first articles were written in Italy but not published until she moved to London in 1877. The first two appeared in the *Edinburgh Review*; one concerned brigands in Sicily and the other the Renaissance polymath Copernicus, who understood the Sun as central to the universe, contrary to the teachings of his time. On the strength of this work the publishers Adam and Charles Black of Edinburgh approached Agnes to write biographies of famous scientists and mathematicians for a new edition of the *Encyclopædia Britannica*. She also contributed articles to the *Dictionary of National Biography* on the same subject.

In London Agnes turned her mind again to astrophysics. She published *A Popular History of Astronomy During the Nineteenth Century* in 1885, and the book became an instant classic. Six further astronomy books followed, and a multitude of articles in which Agnes reported and commented on contemporary research in the field, which she was well-placed to collate given her grasp of languages. Agnes's aim in all of her writing was to reach both a specialist audience and the general reader, and her particular gift was in presenting complex theories in crystal clear language to allow, as she put it, 'the ordinary reader to follow, with intelligent interest, the course of modern astronomical inquiries . . .'

Agnes never married and lived with her brother and sister for all of her adult life, in a house on Redcliffe Square in Brompton. She benefitted from Irish networks in London, and particularly from the friendship of Irish astronomer Margaret Huggins, the wife of astrophysicist William Huggins. The Hugginses had their own private observatory, equipped with the support of the Royal Society, and Margaret and Agnes became lifelong friends, and 'companions in astronomy'. Through Huggins and the growing reputation of her own work, Agnes made a range of other contacts in the world of astronomy, in person and by correspondence. These networks allowed her access to new knowledge including the photographs of planets, comets and nebulae which illustrated her books. The art of photographing such phenomena was in its infancy and these striking images added significantly to the books' popular appeal.

Agnes's dedication and rigour were recognised across the world. She spent two months at the Royal Observatory at the Cape of Good Hope in 1888, where she was able to gain practical experience and view for herself the southern skies. Her published observations on this residency resulted in a job offer from the Royal Observatory in Greenwich, but she declined this opportunity. In 1893 she was awarded the Actonian Prize by the Royal Institution. In her later years she became interested in the new science of X-rays and radioactivity.

Women of Agnes's era were still very much kept on the fringes of scientific enquiry. They were allowed to attend the meetings of the Royal Astronomical Society from 1892, but not to become fellows. Agnes and Margaret Huggins were awarded honorary memberships in 1903, following on from Caroline Herschel, Mary Somerville and Anne Sheepshanks. Agnes was sixty years of age. No woman would be admitted to the fellowship on the same terms as men until 1916.

Agnes died suddenly of pneumonia in 1907, and was buried in the cemetery in Brompton in her family's plot. *The Times* carried her obituary; her *Popular History* had never been out of print in her lifetime. In 1973 a moon crater was named Clerke in her honour by the International Astronomical Union, and in 2002 her biography was published by Cambridge University Press.

LIVE YOUR LIFE BY AGNES

Agnes had no formal education, but rather a deep interest in learning. She was also something of a late starter, publishing her first book at the age of forty-three. Take inspiration from her example – it's never too late to try something new, and anyone may embark on a course of learning.

"Great wars, work, and learning have passed over the world since then, and changed all its fashions. Kings make no seven-day feasts for all-comers now. Queens and princesses, however greedy, do not mine for gold. Chairs tell no tales. Wells work no wonders; and there are no such doings on hills and forests, for the fairies dance no more."

FRANCES BROWNE
GRANNY'S MAGICAL CHAIR
1856

FRANCES BROWNE
WRITER

F rances Browne was not precisely fiery, but she was a determined character. She was born at Stranorlar in County Donegal in 1816, the seventh of twelve children. At the age of eighteen months she lost her sight.

Initially Frances attended Sunday school but did not regularly attend school. She did have lots of social contact, both through her large immediate family and her father's occupation as postmaster in Stranorlar. As a child it seems she already had a gift for language, pestering adults to explain new words to her, listening intently to her siblings read their lessons aloud, and bribing them to read to her by offering to do their chores. As she grew she attended school for periods, and the local schoolmaster lent her books to meet her insatiable appetite for reading. At first she was a fan of fiction – especially the work of Sir Walter Scott – and then she graduated on to history. It's hard to imagine that her mother had a lot of time on her hands, but she did her bit too, instilling a lifelong love of fairy stories and lore in her daughter.

Frances was writing as early as the age of seven. Her first published poetry appeared in 1841, her first collection was published in 1844, and her work was extensively reprinted in the Northern Irish press. Her fame as the 'blind poetess of Ulster' quickly grew. She began to write for *Chambers's Edinburgh Journal* and other magazines as a regular contributor.

Frances's father was an emigration agent, and from a young age Frances had travelled in her mind, tracing routes on a globe with her fingers for a sighted person to name for her. In 1847 she became one of the million or so Irish people to leave the country at the time of the Famine, moving to Edinburgh. She established herself in literary circles there, working through her sister who had travelled with her to facilitate her writing by taking dictation. A move to London followed in 1852. In her later years there Frances lived with a servant and companion, Eliza Hickman.

In London in 1856 Frances published her most famous work, *Granny's Magical Chair*. This collection of stories for children became a bestseller and is still available today. It is a rich collection of fairytales for children, and perhaps drew on Frances's memories of listening to her mother's stories in her childhood, back home in Donegal. It also speaks of her fascination for travel; the characters in the stories seldom remain at home. In some ways it is a quintessentially Irish book, with a landscape of small kingdoms populated by fisherfolk and farmers, shoemakers and blacksmiths, the inhabitants of which travel far and wide.

Frances was highly regarded but never rich, and was dependent on a civil list pension. She found herself in particularly dire financial straits in 1867, when she declared bankruptcy after a publisher defaulted on payment to her. After many years of hard work through ill health, she died at just sixty-three and was buried in Richmond-on-Thames. She left what remained of her estate to Eliza.

LIVE YOUR LIFE BY FRANCES

In 1979, smallpox became the only human disease ever to be completely eradicated. Prior to that point, it had killed, disabled and disfigured millions – including Frances, who lost her sight. It was eradicated through international cooperation on vaccination, coupled with outbreak control until 'herd immunity' was achieved.

In recent years rates of vaccination have taken a serious dip as concerns regarding side-effects have spread, including an infamous and discredited study linking the MMR (measles, mumps, rubella) vaccine to autism. As a result, serious diseases such as measles are seeing a resurgence. The World Health Organisation now identifies vaccine hesitancy as a global health risk.

The risk posed to a child by vaccines is outweighed by many orders of magnitude by the risks posed by the diseases vaccines suppress. Additionally the risk to those who cannot be vaccinated is unacceptable. Please remember Frances and vaccinate your children unless you have specific medical advice not to do so.

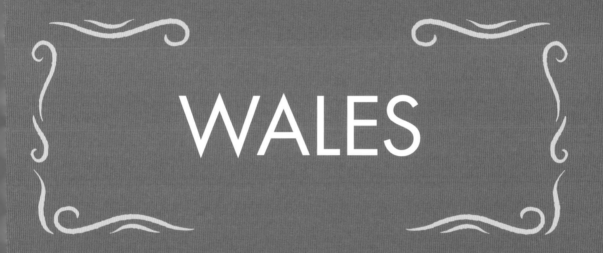

WALES

A 'HERSTORY' OF WALES
POETS AND ABESSES AND SWORD-WIELDING PRINCESSES

PRE-HERSTORY

Continuous human habitation of Wales dates from the period after the last Ice Age and, like Scotland and Ireland, Wales has many Mesolithic, Neolithic and Bronze Age remains. By the Iron Age the area was part of a wider Brittonic Celtic culture that stretched south from the Firth of Forth to meet the broader Celtic world of mainland Europe. At least five Brittonic-speaking tribes occupied modern-day Wales: the Deceangli, the Ordovices, the Demetae, the Silures and the Cornovii.

EARLY HERSTORY

The Romans reached the border of modern Wales in AD 48 and met significant resistance in the form of guerilla warfare. In AD 61, the historian Tacitus records the fall of Anglesey, 'On the coastline, a line of warriors of the opposition was stationed, mainly made up of armed men, amongst them women, with their hair blowing in the wind, while they were carrying torches. Druids were amongst them, shouting terrifying spells, their hands raised towards the heavens . . . At the end of the battle, the Romans were victorious, and the holy oaks of the druids were destroyed.' By around AD 90, Wales was under Roman control, maintained via a network of forts and roads, but much of the way of life of the tribes was preserved nonetheless.

Archaeology allows us to guess at the lives of the Britons in Wales. Graves indicate different ranks in society, from apparent rulers of both sexes – buried with chariots and other significant pieces of art – through elites, warriors, farmers and workers, and slaves. The status of the latter group as chattels is indicated from the presence of gang chains for multiple people recovered in archaeological digs. This was a relatively wealthy society, as the land produced corn and cattle, gold, silver and iron, all of which were exported, and pigs and sheep for meat and clothing. With plentiful metal supplies they plied a trade, with their fellow Celts, as the finest metalsmiths in Europe, creating long swords, exquisite jewellery, spoked wheels and ringed barrels. Even a farming woman might be buried with a wrought bronze mirror.

We also know something of Brittonic people, including women, from Greek and Roman sources, although these war and travel narratives are often unreliable and were written from a position of firmly assumed superiority over the 'Barbarians' their writers described. As well as recording women warriors, Tacitus has it that Welsh people were small and dark, with curly hair. Most other sources describe them as tall and fair-haired, with a fondness among both males and females for jewellery and ornamentation, including gold neck-rings, and intricate hairstyles achieved with the help of lime and other preparations. Women are described as beautiful and the Greek writer Strabo claims that thinness was prized in both sexes and fines imposed for developing a belly. We know that fine cloth and garments were traded to the Romans even before the Roman invasion of Britain.

More broadly, Roman and Greek writers tell us that Celtic women could be powerful, leading war-bands and entire tribes either in their own right or beside their husbands. Strabo describes one tribe in which the position of the sexes relative to each other is 'opposite . . . to how it is with us'. To what degree these recorded Celtic warrior women and leaders were unusual is unclear, as is the degree to which Celtic women enjoyed equality with men.

Our knowledge of religious beliefs is incomplete, but we understand these to have been polytheistic, with both gods and goddesses honoured, and special status possibly given to cycles of the sun and moon, and places such as lakes and mountains, bogs and oak groves. Bog sacrifices of precious items are common, although Wales has yielded few bog bodies to date.

CHRISTIANITY

Under the later Roman empire, Wales became Christian. Women remembered from this period include Saint Elen, a founder of churches. Tradition has it that Elen's father was Romano-British ruler Eudaf Hen/Octavius and her mother the widow of Macsen Wledig/Magnus Maximus, emperor in Britain, Gaul and Spain. The Age of Saints continued for centuries after the Romans withdrew from British territory around AD 410, and many more women appear in the accounts. Fifth-century virgin Saint Adwen was reputedly a daughter of King Brychan of Brycheiniog in Wales and is strongly associated with Cornwall. Canna, daughter of the Breton king Tudur Mawr, presided over communities of monks and nuns in South Wales. Sixth-century Afrelia was a princess of Powys, daughter of Severa Verch Macsen, herself the daughter of the Roman Emperor Maximus, and is said to have founded a monastery. The noblewoman Winifred sought to become a nun in the seventh century, and was decapitated by her suitor Caradoc as a result; a healing spring sprang from the place her head fell. As in Scotland and Ireland, evidence for the activities of these and other early Christian missionaries derives from later sources, and little evidence remains of their religious buildings or settlements, but their existence in legend and later accounts is a tantalising glimpse of the broad-ranging and influential activities of women.

MEDIEVAL HERSTORY

As Roman influence waned and Anglo-Saxon power grew, widespread Brittonic Celtic culture in mainland Britain fragmented and the Welsh people began to develop an identity in their own right. By the eighth century the Welsh language remained linked to languages spoken in the 'Hen Ogedd' (Old North), Cornwall and Brittany but was developing as a distinct entity. (Breton and Welsh survive into the modern day and there have been attempts to revive Cornish, but the language of Hen Ogedd did not survive the disappearance of its various kingdoms into Anglo-Saxon and Pictish territories.)

A number of kingdoms formed across Wales, but none was able to unite the whole territory for long. War between the kingdoms, pressure from England and then Norman invasion saw Wales come under the control of Edward I of England in 1284 with the Statute of Rhuddlan. History focuses on the Welsh princes in this period; research suggests that this is to do a disservice to Welsh women, who played active parts in politics, in battle and in wider life. The story of Nest ferch Rhys (see page 161), has perhaps promoted the 'damsel in distress' model of the medieval woman; by contrast Gwenllian (see page 165) led her people to war and Senana ferch Caradog, the great-great granddaughter of Owain Gwynedd, petitioned Henry III for the release of her husband Grufudd ap Llewelyn. Senana and Henry agreed a settlement that included two of Senana's sons as hostages, and the loyalty of a number of other Welsh families. These are perhaps unusual examples; women appear most commonly in sources as mothers and wives, and we should not fall into a trap of underestimating the importance of those roles in contrast to women operating in the more traditionally 'male' political sphere. They do retreat from religious life in this era; by the thirteenth century religious seclusion appears rather more to be a punishment for women than a desired vocation, or at best a protection of last resort, for example for a widow.

The Laws of Hywel Dda, a collection of texts from around the tenth to the thirteenth centuries, has a fair bit to say on women. The relevant sections cover the various settlements payable to a woman and her family on marriage, which were calculated based on her material wealth. These were important as most crimes against a woman could be settled with a fee calculated in terms of these payments – this system of paid compensation for crime was rather more a feature of law in Celtic communities than in English and French-speaking areas. Rape could be proven by a woman taking relics in her right hand and the penis of the accused in her left and swearing to the rape; thereafter fees were payable. Welsh women were entitled to compensation if their husband committed adultery; if he did so on three occasions, the wronged wife was entitled to a divorce – any monies owing were however forfeited if the woman chose not to leave the adulterer. If a woman was found guilty of consensual extramarital sex, her husband could leave her without owing her compensation and instead could seek compensation from the man with whom she had committed her crime. Women could leave their husband without losing their property in the event the husband suffered from leprosy or bad breath, as you will surely agree is only fair on the latter count.

The Statute of Rhuddlan ushered in English power in Wales, and it made specific provisions regarding women. In contrast to the previous Welsh law, it disinherited illegitimate sons and recognised daughters as heirs in the absence of sons. In some ways this appears a step forward for women, but it also barred Englishmen married to Welsh women from bearing office in Wales. This acted as a disincentive for Welsh–English intermarriage and thereby barred Welsh women, and in turn their wider families, from access to power. It's interesting to reflect on whether this represents a perception of Welsh women as effective political operators who must be curtailed.

ENGLAND AND WALES

Welsh culture and language continued to flourish through centuries of English power. Rebellions in the 1200s, 1300s and 1400s failed, and the last of these, led by Owain Glyndwr, resulted in the passing of the Penal Laws against Wales, which prohibited Welsh people from bearing arms, holding office or living in fortified towns. As with the Statute of Rhuddlan, these prohibitions also applied to Englishmen married to Welsh women. Welsh troops were extensively active during the Wars of the Roses, and ultimate victors the Tudors enjoyed a level of popular Welsh support. Tudor King Henry VIII passed the Laws in Wales Acts between 1535 and 1542, which sought to integrate Wales with England. These Acts abolished Welsh law and banned the Welsh language from official contexts.

While Welsh people had become legally indistinguishable from the English, Welsh of course remained the language of most of the population. Women still used their traditional patronymic names in addition to or instead of the English-style surnames that were supposed to be used. A Welsh translation of the Bible in 1588 boosted the language in literary expression.

CIVIL WAR

In the seventeenth century Wales tended to support the Royalist side in the Wars of the Three Kingdoms. It might be fair to observe that most people in Wales were not strongly disposed towards either side (infamously, drops were made in the country of leaflets in English, a language most people could not speak or read), but generally they were directed by landowners' allegiances. Among the landowning classes, it's notable that husbands and wives did not necessarily support the same side. One example we know of a marital rift concerns Anne, wife of John Bodvile of Anglesey. John Bodvile became a colonel in Charles I's army, while Anne was a supporter of parliament. John removed their children and placed them in the care of his mother to ensure that Anne was unable to influence their religious and political views.

Another mother wrote to her son in concern that he might join the parliamentary army. 'I do suffer more pain for the ways you take . . . than I ever did to bring you into the world,' wrote the Countess of Denbigh to her son Basil, in 1642. 'I hope you will never take up arms against the king for that would be too heavy a burden for me to bear.'

As in previous conflicts, Welsh troops were important, particularly to King Charles. Losses were heavy, and included women followers of the army. At Naseby in June 1645 at least one hundred women died and others had their faces mutilated. The parliamentary army justified this atrocity by claiming that the women were speaking an incomprehensible language and so they assumed them to be Irish. Which would of course make slaughtering a bunch of women just dandy – an act the army had already undertaken at Wexford and Drogheda in Ireland.

COAL AND NON-CONFORMISM

In eighteenth-century Wales, Methodism took a firm hold, and various religious revivals into the twentieth century cemented non-conformist religion in Wales. The status of Methodist women was subordinate to that of men, but women did perform or share in important functions of worship and church life. A notable figure in Welsh Methodism was Englishwoman Selina, Countess of Huntingdon, who helped finance early Methodism and became the first principal of Trevecca College in Powys, which trained Methodist ministers. In the early days of Methodism, female preaching was permitted, but after 1800, women were discouraged from preaching, particularly to mixed congregations. Many women remained determined to carry on nonetheless, particularly in overseas missions and other evangelical activity. Welsh was resurgent as the language of Wales' non-conformist worship, and Sunday schools helped a large part of the population become literate in the language.

The industrial revolution changed the face of Wales from the end of the eighteenth century onwards, as iron ore, limestone and coal deposits in the south-east saw the establishment of ironworks and coalmines. Development of these industries was male-dominated, but a number of women were also active. 'Mother of the coal industry' Lucy Thomas took over running her husband's coalmine at Merthyr in 1833 and increased the value of the business more than tenfold, despite the fact she could neither read nor write. Lady Charlotte Guest (see page 181) took control of her own husband's ironworks – the largest in the world – when he died in 1852. She is remembered both as the translator of the Mabinogion and for her philanthropic works focused on workers in the area.

Many thousands more women were of course instrumental in the success of industry in Wales, as workers in their own right and as the wives and mothers of miners and ironworkers. Mothers and wives were as much slaves to the shifts of mines and ironworks as their husbands and sons, on hand to feed them and bathe them whenever they came home. This was back-breaking work with no modern labour-saving devices and, when combined with the risks of birthing large families, resulted in a mortality rate for women in the 24 to 44 age bracket in south-east Wales that was actually higher than for men well into the twentieth century.

THE BLUE BOOKS

In 1847 hard-working Welsh women everywhere were dealt a low blow with the publication of the 'Blue Books', a report by three English commissioners sent to Wales supposedly to review the state of education. The commissioners went considerably further than enquiry into the classroom and decided also to address the moral and religious fibre of the Welsh people. They found this to be lacking, particularly in terms of Welsh women:

> They learn anything but delicacy of thought and feeling and when they grow to womanhood and marry, they know next to nothing of the management of a house . . .

> As wives they are most slovenly and improvident, and as mothers, ignorant, and injudicious.

These charming gentlemen naturally spoke no Welsh and based their conclusions on the opinions of Anglican clergymen, who were predisposed to disapprove of the predominantly non-conformist Welsh.

There was an outcry and women's magazine *Y Gymraes* (The Welsh Woman) was founded by non-conformist minister Evan Jones as a response to 'Brad y Llyfrau Gleision', or 'the Treachery of the Blue Books'. *Y Gymraes* promoted religion, marriage and morality, with housekeeping and cookery advice. Riveting as this sounds, it lasted a mere two years and the women of Wales had to wait another twenty before poet and writer Sarah Jane Rees ('Cranogwen') began to publish *Y Frythones*, or The Female Briton. It ran for twelve years, when *Y Gymraes* was again revived, this time under a female editor, and ran until the 1930s.

Sarah Jane Rees was also active in another reaction to the Blue Books – the Temperance movement. This was in part intended to answer the accusations of the Book commissioners, but many women were also motivated by the political ends of protecting family income that might otherwise be drunk away, and reducing domestic violence, which was exacerbated by alcoholism. The campaigning activity undertaken by women in the Temperance movement gave many a taste for political activism which they would soon apply to a new cause – votes for women.

THE WOMEN'S FREEDOM LEAGUE

In 1909 the Women's Freedom League was established in Swansea. It was a non-violent campaigning body established to 'secure for Women the Parliamentary Vote on the same terms as it is or may be granted to men; to use the power thus obtained to establish equality of rights and opportunities between the sexes; and to promote the social and industrial well-being of the community'. Other Welsh women wished to pursue more violent action. Margaret Haig Mackworth (née Thomas) blew up a postbox in Newport, to show how strongly she felt about votes for women. This earned her a sentence in prison, but she went on hunger strike and was released after five days.

The campaign was overshadowed by the First World War, and women were not granted the vote until 1918 – even then it was only granted to those over thirty, depriving many who had worked in munitions factories and the fields during the war their enfranchisement. Neither were women able to take up seats in the House of Lords – Margaret Haig Mackworth tried to inherit her father's seat in 1918 and was refused. Playwright George Bernard Shaw commented that her attempt demonstrated the 'imbecility of the male sex as never before'.

Another Welsh woman did enjoy success in the Lords, if not as a member. Former suffragette Elizabeth Andrews was invited to make a speech in the House of Lords in 1919 as a member of the Labour party. She testified on the physical strain, injury and early deaths suffered by women in mining communities as a result of endless lifting and carrying of hot water for baths. Elizabeth's speech was instrumental in the installation of pit-head baths at colleries, which became compulsory in 1924.

RIGHTS FOR WOMEN

All women above the voting age of twenty-one were able to vote in the general election of 1929. Three women stood for election to parliament in Wales and one succeeded. She was Megan Lloyd George, daughter of the former prime minister David Lloyd George, and she was elected Liberal MP for Anglesey. A keen advocate for Welsh, and for women's rights, Megan would hold her seat through a further three elections.

Welsh women had many battles on their hands throughout the twentieth century. The right for married women to work was hard-fought, as was access to birth control. Women were active in many more general actions too. They took to the streets during the General Strike of 1926 and hunger-marched with men to London in the 1930s. During the Miners' Strike in the 1980s they opposed the closure of the pits of South Wales. They marched to Greenham Common to protest the nuclear threat.

CONTEMPORARY WALES

The history of women in Wales has only received serious attention since the 1960s and, for many time periods, as late as the 1980s. Many academics are now making up for lost time, accessing local and national collections of records and artefacts including the work of women's hands from ancient times to the modern day. The following stories of badass Welsh sisters seek to underline that women have always been more than a match for the 'land of our fathers'.

"having from her infancy dedicated herself solely to the service of God, in her riper years, being violently pressed by a young prince to marriage, to free herself from his solicitations and those of her family, she secretly stole away from her father's house in a disguise . . ."

HUGH THOMAS RECORDS TRADITIONS OF ELUNED
IN THE LATE SEVENTEENTH CENTURY
HARLEIAN MANUSCRIPT 4,181

ELUNED

HOLY WOMAN

Strong-minded Eluned was born in the fifth century or early sixth century, one of a very large family. Her father Brychan was king of Brycheiniog in the south of Wales, born in Ireland and, according to tradition, married three times in Wales. With his wives Prawst, Banhadlwedd and Gwladys he produced somewhere between twelve and sixty-three children, with many chroniclers settling on twenty-four. The family was a holy one; Brychan held his lands under Roman authority, and he was an early convert to Christianity. His many children were evangelists for the new faith, setting out to convert the communities of Cornwall and Devon in particular. Many were sainted for their efforts, and this may have led others to claim descent from this holy bunch.

Eluned's faith was strong from a young age and she determined to dedicate her life to God. This thwarted the plans of the pagan Welsh prince who wished to marry her, and Eluned ran away in order to avoid his advances. She stopped in Llan Ddew, Llanfilo and Llechfaen, but in each place was taken as a beggar or even a thief, and turned out or forced to sleep in the street. She could find no place to settle until she reached Slwch Tump, where the local lord offered her sanctuary and she could build her cell. She seems to have prospered there, supported by the charity of said local lord, and, according to Hugh Thomas, she soon took up prophecy. In short order she predicted disaster for Llan Ddew, Llanfilo and Llechfaen, which does rather suggest that early Christian saints were not above a spot of vengeance. Llan Ddew would be chastised by God. Llanfilo, where Eluned had been accused of being a thief, would be plagued with thieves in perpetuity. Llechfaen would be plagued with envy, so that the villagers would continually be involved in disputes with one another.

Lesson: be nice to passing saints.

All this vengeance and – presumably – prayer came to an end when Eluned's would-be lover pursued her to her cell. She fled from him, and he killed her by decapitation. Her head rolled down the hill and hit a stone; a healing spring burst from the place it lay and later a yew tree grew there.

In the detail of the decapitation and the spring, Eluned's story closely reflects that of Saint Winifred's, indicating either a significant level of psychopathy among spurned Welsh princes, enthusiasm for anti-pagan propaganda among Christian chroniclers, or perhaps a bit of both. The well at Slwch was named after Eluned in perpetuity and considered a holy and healing place of pilgrimage for centuries thereafter. Its first mention in written record comes in 1152, when its grant to the Prior of Brecon by Bernard, Bishop of Brecon, was confirmed by his successor David. The chapel fell into ruin after the Reformation, although some walls were still standing in 1698. Today the remains of four terraced platforms may be seen, where presumably the chapel complex stood. It is a scheduled ancient monument in recognition of the potential of its archaeology to enhance our understanding of the organisation of medieval church complexes.

The fifteenth-century chronicler William Worcester wrote that Eluned's remains were housed with the Benedictine nuns at Usk. Perhaps Eluned found a community of sisters in her death.

LIVE YOUR LIFE BY ELUNED

You don't want to be cursed for a lack of charity, much less bring down the wrath of a higher power on your whole community. If you can afford to support a local foodbank or other charity by direct debit, please do. If money's an issue, charities can always use donations or volunteers.

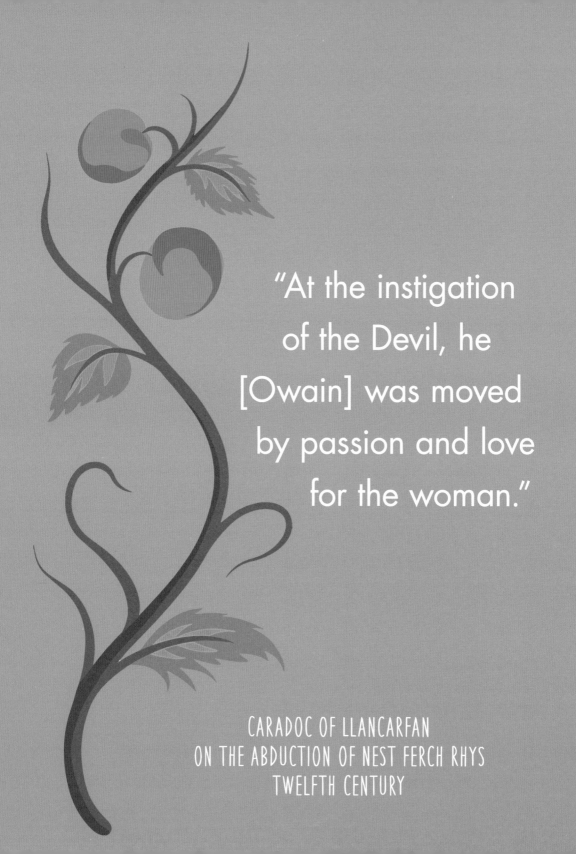

"At the instigation of the Devil, he [Owain] was moved by passion and love for the woman."

CARADOC OF LLANCARFAN
ON THE ABDUCTION OF NEST FERCH RHYS
TWELFTH CENTURY

NEST FERCH RHYS
PRINCESS

When you were little, did you ever pick on another sibling, claiming they were adopted, while nursing a secret jealous suspicion that, really, they were the favoured child? If so, then thank your lucky stars that you didn't live in twelfth-century Wales, when parents and other family members regularly had to pick a child to give as a hostage to secure the release of an adult or even a more important sibling. That's 'important' in the dynastic sense, of course, because naturally no parent ever has favourites.*

Nest ferch Rhys was born around 1080, the only legitimate daughter of Rhys ap Tewdwr, the last king of Deheubarth and his wife Gwladys, the daughter of Powys king Rhiwallon ap Cynfyn. On her father's death Nest was taken as hostage by William Rufus, the third son of William the Conqueror. In a bit of dishonourable conduct at court, Nest then became the latest conquest of Henry Beauclerc, William Rufus's brother, who became Henry I in 1100. She bore him an illegitimate son in 1103, to add to his tally of twenty or so children borne by his mistresses. A medieval manuscript in the British Library contains a comical picture of the two naked in bed, still wearing their crowns, but it's less jolly to reflect that Nest was around fourteen at the time of the seduction. When Henry was done with Nest he married her off to Gerald FitzWalter of Windsor, Norman constable of Pembroke Castle. Their children would later play a part in

*Yes they do.

the Norman invasion of Ireland and the FitzGeralds would become one of the most influential families in that country.

Nest's fame rests not on her status as matriarch, however, but rather on the fact of her abduction and rape by Owain ap Cadwgan, Prince of Powys, which has earned her a reputation as a Welsh Helen of Troy. A number of places lay claim to being the location of Owain's attack, which is inconvenient for our purposes if not for those of the tourist industry. Nest was attacked at one of:

- Cenarth Bychan (perhaps Cilgerran Castle in Pembrokeshire), Nest's home, where Owain may have dug his way in.
- Carew Castle, where tradition has it that Nest encouraged Gerald to escape via a long-drop toilet and stayed to face Owain, who had dug his way in or scaled the walls and set the castle on fire.
- An undisclosed location where Nest and Gerald were attending an eisteddfod (cultural festival) during a truce with Owain's dad Cadwgan ap Bleddyn and, we presume, no digging was necessary on Owain's part.
- Somewhere else entirely, with or without digging and/or toilet-related escapes.

Accounts vary as to Owain's motivations. Various chroniclers have it that (a) he had fallen in love with Nest, who was quite the beauty (b) she was a useful hostage as a daughter of Deheubarth or (c) a bit of both. To be completely radical, this book will dispense with such speculation and simply observe that men have been viewing women as objects for millennia and this behaviour urgently needs to end.

Nest was carried off with her children and held by Owain, to much Norman and Welsh consternation. After numerous attacks on Owain and his father, first the children and then Nest herself were released. Owain and Cadwgan sought exile in Ireland, hopefully to reflect on their poor choices in life and parenting failures respectively.

Around 1112 Gerald of Windsor killed Owain ap Cadwgan, who had returned from exile, become Prince of Powys on his father's death and joined King Henry's forces against a Welsh uprising. Gerald died at some time around 1120 or shortly thereafter, and Nest married again, to one of his constables.

In the centuries that passed after Nest's death, chroniclers attributed a couple of sons to her by Owain and a couple of extra lovers, and in this way worked their way round to thinking that she had probably connived at her abduction in the way, you know, women do.

LIVE YOUR LIFE BY NEST

Believe the woman.

"Ddail achos Gwenllian!"

"Revenge for Gwenllian!"

LEGENDARY MEDIEVAL WELSH BATTLE CRY

GWENLLIAN FERCH GRUFFYDD

WARRIOR

Gwenllian ferch Gruffydd was descended from a pretty kick-ass line of people, including no less a figure than Brian Bóruma, the High King credited in legend with forcing the Vikings from Ireland. There was little apparent dilution of this spirit by the time Gwenllian – his great-great-great granddaughter – was born in Ynys Môn (Anglesey) in the late 1090s. Perhaps the fact she was the youngest of eight children helped Gwenllian develop a core of steel; she wouldn't be the first small sibling to have to fight for her place in the world.

Gwenllian's parents were Gruffydd ap Cynan, ruler of Gwynedd, and Angharad ferch Owain, daughter of a noble dynasty in north-west Wales. Angharad had a reputation for beauty, eloquence and queenly bearing, and accounts suggest that her last-born daughter inherited these in full measure. Gruffydd, on the other hand, was a fighter who had seized his throne over numerous rival princes and spent a dozen years in captivity after the Norman invasion of Wales. Perhaps he saw fit to ensure his daughter's education included the use of arms.

In or around 1113, Gruffydd ap Rhys ventured to Gwynedd to meet Gwenllian's father. Gruffydd was a son of the Dinefwr dynasty and ruler of Deheubarth, the realms of South Wales, but most of his territory had fallen under Norman control. After some years in exile, he sought Gruffydd ap Cynan's support in his ongoing struggles with Henry I of England. There is some suggestion that the older Gruffydd planned to do the younger man harm while in his power; the Prince of Deheubarth did, however, escape unscathed . . . but not alone.

He and Gwenllian had become involved and the pair eloped from Gwynedd, returning to Gruffydd's family seat of Dinefwr. There they began a family that would eventually reach double digits.

Following the marriage there was a time of relative stability in Wales, and in 1121 or 1122, Gruffydd made peace with Henry I and received control of a portion of his kingdom in return. This was an uneasy truce, however, and Gwenllian and Gruffydd enjoyed little security. The family was under constant Norman pressure and was regularly displaced, with Gruffydd exiled again to Ireland at one point. Both Gruffydd and Gwenllian engaged in strikes against the colonists, operating from a series of strongholds in mountainous and forested regions. Some accounts have them plundering Norman wealth to redistribute among their own people.

In 1135 Stephen de Blois seized the throne from his cousin the Empress Matilda, who had succeeded her father Henry I after her only legitimate brother drowned in a disaster at sea. The Welsh princes saw the opportunity that war between Stephen and Matilda presented. The 'Great Revolt' began in South Wales in 1136, with success for Hywel ap Maredudd at the Battle of Llwchwr. Gruffydd ap Rhys went to his father-in-law in Gwynedd to seek the older Gruffydd's support for a rising of his own. While he was gone, Maurice de Londres, Lord of Kidwelly, and other Normans moved to attack Deheubarth. Gwenllian was forced to respond. She gathered her army ready for war.

In a battle fought near Kidwelly Castle, the Deheubarth army was defeated and Gwenllian was captured and beheaded, apparently as a deterrent to others. Her sons Maelgwyn and Morgan were also killed.

Gwenllian's death served to help rally others in Wales to rise against the Normans. Gwenllian's brothers Owain and Cadwaladr were among these. Owain would go on to become the greatest of the North Welsh princes, only surpassed by his own grandson fifty years later. Her son Rhys would succeed his father to become one of the most successful rulers of Deheubarth, and the main power in Wales after his uncle Owain's death.

It is said that Gwenllian's personal legacy lived on in a war cry, in a Welsh lullaby and in the place name *Maes Gwenllian*, which commemorates the field where she died. It has even been claimed that she may have been the author of the four branches of *The Mabinogion* (see page 183). More distantly, Gwenllian's habit of seizing Norman goods and money for distribution among her own people is said to have inspired the character of Maid Marion in legends of Robin Hood, J. R. R. Tolkein may have based his shield-maiden Eówyn of Rohan on her in *The Lord of the Rings*, and she may be a source for Guinevere in Arthurian legend.

Whether these characters are truly associated with Gwenllian or not, she was remarkable in her own right. She is the only medieval Welsh woman we know of to lead an army into battle. You don't get much more badass than that.

LIVE YOUR LIFE BY GWENLLIAN

In contrast to the general portrayal of Gwenllian as a badass heroine who paid the ultimate price for brave defence of her country, a chronicle of the 1100s rather randomly asserts that, instead, she murdered her husband Gruffydd. That she did not do this is relatively clear, for the simple reason that Gruffydd outlived her by some measure. Perhaps the monks of Worcester who composed the *Chronicon ex chronicis* had trouble imagining a woman riding into battle.

Remember Gwenllian and endeavour to make your own mind up about people rather than relying on second-hand judgements. There are two sides to any story. From politics to personal relationships, it's always worth doing your research.

"Good people,
you are mistaken;
I am the Protestant
whore."

NELL GWYN CORRECTS
THE MISAPPREHENSION OF THE PEOPLE OF OXFORD THAT SHE
IS KING CHARLES II'S *OTHER* MISTRESS, IN 1661. RECALLED BY
PHILIBERT, COMTE DE GRAMONT, IN *MEMOIRES*
1710

ELEANOR 'NELL' GWYN

ACTRESS

A girl's gotta do what a girl's gotta do. Nell Gwyn took her natural endowments – wit, looks and (one suspects) an ability to tolerate a lot in terms of male ego – and got on with making the best of the fairly poor cards dealt her.

We don't know precisely when Nell was born, with sources differing by some eight or ten years between the early 1640s and 1650. Nell might have chosen not to clear up the mystery; as they say, it's not polite to ask a lady her age. Further mystery surrounds her parentage. 'It's a wise bairn kens its faither,' as the saying goes, but of course maternal lineage is rather easier to track. Her mother was Ellen, known variously as 'Old Madam' or 'Old Ma Gwyn', who was born in 1623 in St Martin in the Fields, a parish covering a large swathe of London around Covent Garden. The story goes that Ellen liked a drink, and drowned upon falling into water by her house near Chelsea at the age of fifty-six.

Nell's father is reported to have belonged to an ancient family in Wales. There's no particularly reliable evidence that this was the case, but it's handy for the purposes of this book, as it was handy for Nell's own purposes when she got her own arms and went with a design similar to that of the Gwynnes of Llansannor in Wales. Tradition has it that Nell was born in Hereford, in Pipe Well Lane, which was renamed Gwynne Street in the 1800s to commemorate these associations. Herefordshire is on the border with Wales, lending further weight to the Welsh theory, given also the Welsh origins of Nell's surname. But Welsh, English or whatever else he might have been, Nell's dad was lacking in the responsibility department and had made himself scarce by the time of Nell's childhood in Covent Garden. Her mother made shift to support herself, Nell and her older daughter Rose by running a brothel.

It's depressingly possible that Nell's mother used her as a child prostitute, and accounts suggest that she spent time not only in her mother's establishment, but also in a neighbouring facility run by one Madam Ross. Nell herself claimed she was never anything other than a barmaid. However, the diarist Samuel Pepys records in 1667 that during a row with another woman, Nell is supposed to have said, 'I was but one man's whore, though I was brought up in a bawdy-house to fill strong waters to the guests; and you are a whore to three or four, though a Presbyter's praying daughter!' Whether she was telling the truth or not, you've got to give it to Nell that she had style in her put-downs.

Nell's early years were spent in the Protectorate of Oliver Cromwell, when frivolity was frowned upon. After the Restoration of Charles II to the throne in 1660, however, frivolity was all the rage. Charles got on with getting licences issued for two theatre companies, and made it legal for women to act on the stage for good measure. Nell's theatre career began in the Theatre on Brydges Street (later the Theatre Royal, Drury Lane) when it opened in 1663 – but not on the stage. Instead she had a job selling oranges and other sweet treats to the patrons. She was by this means exposed not only to the workings of the theatre but also to high society via the patrons, up to and including the king himself. She was also fairly exposed in another sense, given the scanty costume she wore.

Nell didn't last long as an orange-girl – she was destined for greater things. The actor Charles Hart and theatre owner Thomas Killigrew established a school for young actors and actresses, which Nell joined. Her debut on the stage cannot be established for sure – a 'Mrs Nell' appears in cast lists as early as 1664 – but by 1665 she had risen to be sufficiently well-known that Samuel Pepys mentions her in his diary by her first name only. Pepys found Nell 'pretty' and 'witty' but he did not consider she had the chops for serious acting. Instead, she had a gift for comedy, and the Restoration was a golden era for these. She became synonymous with 'gay couple' comedies based on witty lovers scoring points off one another. Often she played opposite Charles Hart, who had become her lover.

Theatres were shut down across London when the Plague struck the city. The king and his court left for the cleaner air of the countryside, and Nell travelled with his retinue as a player. After her return to London she enjoyed perhaps the greatest triumph of her career, appearing in *Secret Love, or The Maiden Queen* by John Dryden. In the play Nell appeared on stage in breeches, reprising a role she was reputed to have played under her own steam in her youth – that of a young gallant. Such antics of course ensured she caught the eye of every gentleman in the audience; one of these, Charles Sackville, Lord Buckhurst, was able to make Nell an offer to keep her in some style, and she became his mistress. Pepys reported that he gave her £100 a year, a fortune at the time. Nell briefly gave up acting during this liaison, but was back on the stage by 1667.

At some time in 1668, Nell began an affair with the king. The story goes that the two met at a play; the king sat in the next box to Nell and flirted with her. At the end of the night Nell and her companion went to supper with the king, whereupon Charles discovered he didn't have a penny on him, and Nell stood the company their meal.

Nell's affair with her own 'Charles the Third' (after Charles Hart and Charles Sackville) lasted a number of years. She still acted, but reduced her commitments on the stage in order to devote her time to the king. She gave birth to a son, Charles, in 1670. During the early years of the affair, there was little to indicate antagonism with the king's other mistresses, but Nell did engage in a significant rivalry with a later mistress, Louise de Kérouaille. Nell called Louise a range of nicknames including 'Squintabella' and Louise made her own thoughts on the 'orange wench' clear, but it does appear that the women occasionally offered one another companionship.

Once recovered from Charles's birth, Nell was back on stage for her last season. She moved into a brick townhouse on Pall Mall owned by the crown and campaigned for it to be made over to her, which it finally was in 1676. In 1671 she gave birth to her second child, James, who died at school in France when he was ten years old. Her elder son lived to adulthood, being made Baron of Heddington and Earl of Buford in the same year the Pall Mall house was made over to Nell. Tradition has it that Nell wangled this title for him with characteristic style; during a visit from the king, she is supposed to have said, 'Come here, you little bastard, and say hello to your father.' When the king protested, Nell's retort was, 'Your Majesty has given me no other name by which to call him.' Unlikely to be true, this is still a great story and indicative of the wit with which Nell was generally credited.

With her wit or otherwise, Nell also had the grant of a house in Windsor and a summer residence in the area where Kings Cross Station now stands. In 1684, a year before his death, Charles made Nell's son Duke of St Albans, with a grant of £1,000 a year. He remembered Nell herself on his deathbed, begging his brother James, 'Let not poor Nelly starve.' James was as good as his word, paying off Nell's debts and giving her a pension of £1,500 a year.

In 1687, Nell suffered a series of strokes that left her confined to bed. She made her will and died of a further stroke on 14 November; she was no more than forty-five years old and her death was ascribed to syphilis. She remembered her humble beginnings to the end, leaving a bequest to the poor of her parish and funds to release debtors from prison.

LIVE YOUR LIFE BY NELL

Nelly was a mistress of the one-liner and quip, but in reality put-downs can sting. They're not always easy to handle either, since they are easily disguised as wit or even as back-handed compliments, and they are common in unhealthy relationships. If you do find yourself on the receiving end of a painful put-down, what do you do?

One strategy is to push the put-down back at the person making it. Repeat what they said, and that it came across to you as a put-down. Ask them what they meant by it. By this point most people will apologise; if, however, the person insists on telling you the put-down was a joke, or that you're making too much of it, tell them you didn't appreciate it and you don't want it to happen again. If it does, you might want to think about removing that person from your life.

ELEANOR CHARLOTTE BUTLER AND SARAH PONSONBY

'ROMANTIC FRIENDS'

L ater in their lives Eleanor Butler and Sarah Ponsonby would be known as the 'Ladies of Llangollen,' resident in Plas Newydd outside the Welsh village of Llangollen in Denbighshire. They did not, however, originate in Wales. Instead they fled there in search of freedom.

Eleanor Butler was born in 1739 to the Butler family of Kilkenny Castle in Ireland – the Earls of Ormond. Eleanor was sent to a convent in France for her education and when she returned her family found her over-educated, over-fond of books and over-quick with her wit.

Eleanor met thirteen-year-old Sarah (or Sally) Ponsonby in 1768 and the two women formed an instant bond. Sarah was the orphaned daughter of Irish parliamentarian Chambré Brabazon Ponsonby (note that name down for anyone expecting a baby soon) and his second wife Louisa Lyons. When she and Eleanor met, Sarah was living with her late father's cousins Sir William and Lady Betty Fownes in Woodstock, and attending a Miss Parke's School in Kilkenny.

Eleanor and Sarah were united by a shared love of French philosophy and romantic novels. They also shared a horror of being forced into marriage against their will, and instead they conceived of a desire to live together in 'retirement'. This term indicated a step back from society to live instead in an appropriately romantic rural location, where study, gardening, art and such improving activity would be the order of the day. In the late 1770s, the pair absconded, Sarah climbing through a window with the help of her servant Mary Caryll. Their families pursued them and the elopement failed. This did not dent their determination,

"GLYN CAFAILLGAROCH, in the Cambrian tongue,

In ours, the VALE OF FRIENDSHIP, let this spot

Be named; where, faithful to a low-roofed Cot,

On Deva's banks, ye have abode so long;

Sisters in love, a love allowed to climb,

Even on this earth, above the reach of Time!"

'TO THE LADY E. B. AND THE HON. MISS P.'
WILLIAM WORDSWORTH
1824

and eventually the families gave up. Eleanor and Sarah made their way to Wales and sent for Mary Caryll to join them.

Eleanor and Sarah undertook a tour of the Welsh countryside with the aim of locating an appropriate idyll in which to set up home. They rented a home in the village of Llangollen for a time, and then in 1780 moved into a small cottage outside the village called *Pen y Maes* (the head of the field), which they rechristened *Plas Newydd*, or New Mansion.

Plas Newydd stood in a perfectly romantic location with a mountain backdrop and a ravine nearby, and soon its simple architecture was improved upon by Eleanor and Sarah, who installed panelling of Welsh oak, arches and stained glass windows in the Gothic fashion of the day. Interiors were gifted by friends or salvaged from other fine houses and churches. Guests were entertained in a fine library, loyal Mary was joined by further maids, a footman and a gardener to attend to the ornate grounds, and a dairy was added to the little estate. The women had only a limited income from their families to support them, and later a civil list pension, and their levels of expenditure led them into debt on various occasions until they were rescued by the kindness of various friends.

The Ladies' idealised romantic lifestyle attracted many of the thinkers and socialites of the day. They were visited by the Duke of Wellington, Percy Bysshe Shelley, Lord Byron, Sir Walter Scott and Josiah Wedgewood. Lady Caroline Lamb, Anna Seward, Arthur Wellesley, Thomas De Quincey and Robert Southey all sat in the library at one time or another; William Wordsworth composed the sonnet seen opposite in those glorious gardens.

While the Ladies attracted some comment for their eccentricity and good deeds, it might be noted that they attracted little scandal for their relationship. Perhaps their 'romantic friendship' was taken at face value; Anna Seward certainly describes them as an example of 'chaste provinciality'. Perhaps they conformed in other ways. Their respectability contrasts with the treatment of other women of the era who were in apparent lesbian relationships. The sculptor Anne Seymour Damer, for example, attracted rather more negative comment for her relationships with the actress Elizabeth Farren and the author Mary Berry (not the one from *Bake Off*, she's an impressive older lady but not quite that old). Damer, the target of such satire as *A Sapphick Epistle from Jack Cavendish to the Honourable and most Beautiful, Mrs D—*, perhaps challenged the status quo through pursuit of an occupation generally reserved for males, whereas the

Ladies of Llangollen stuck to more 'feminine' pursuits. Landowner Anne Lister of Halifax visited the Ladies; she also suffered harassment for her sexuality but, again, operated in a commercial world more commonly reserved for males and so was particularly visible.

Despite their love for art and finer things, the Ladies were adamant that they wished to have no portraits painted. This apparently did not deter Glamorgan Pottery from producing its 'Llangollen' blueware plate design, showing two women on horseback in the landscape around Plas Newydd. Another plate design, from William Adams of Stoke, is called 'Ladies of Llangollen' and shows the two women in their customary riding habits talking to a fisherman. The women were tricked into a more detailed portrait when Lady Parker visited them in 1829. She arranged for her mother to distract Eleanor and Sarah while she sketched their faces covertly. Eleanor – who died that same year – was completely blind and Lady Parker was able to sketch her full face; Sarah is shown in the sketch in profile. After Sarah's death in 1831 Lady Parker drew her rough up into a fully worked picture of the Ladies in their library and sold copies for charity. That portrait was then pirated to create a more famous image of the Ladies, printed by James Henry Lynch and distributed on the mass market as a souvenir image, postcard and book cover.

Mary died in 1809, Eleanor in 1829 and Sarah in 1831. The three women are buried in the same plot and share a marker.

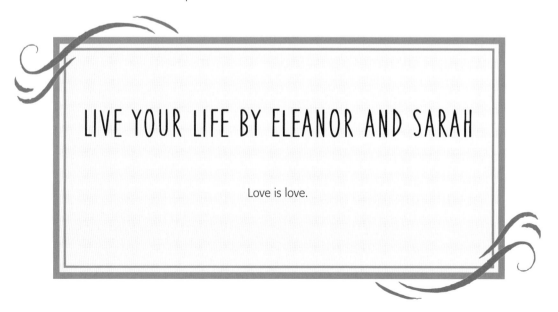

LIVE YOUR LIFE BY ELEANOR AND SARAH

Love is love.

BETSI CADWALADR

NURSE

lizabeth Cadwaladr – known as Betsi and sometimes Beti – was born in 1789 at Llanycil, near Bala in Wales, and grew up on Pen Rhiw Farm. She was one of sixteen children and her mother died when she was just five.

Betsi's father Dafydd was a Methodist preacher and Betsi would have known the famous story of Mary Jones, a fifteen-year-old Welsh girl who walked twenty-six miles barefoot to buy a copy of the Welsh Bible from the clergyman Thomas Charles, inspiring the foundation of the British and Foreign Bible Society. Mary was a near-contemporary of Betsi's and a national icon, and perhaps the link to her helped Betsi feel that she had found purpose in her life upon receiving her very own copy of the Bible from Reverend Charles.

Betsi's first employment was locally in Wales as a maid, where, as well as her tasks, she learned English and to play the harp. While this sounds a reasonable experience, Betsi was not happy and absconded via the old trick of a rope of tied sheets. She made her way to Liverpool and found work as a servant there, changing her name to Davis. Stints at home in Wales and then in London followed.

Perhaps Betsi had developed itchy feet on her travels, because she undertook considerable travel in the various positions she occupied over the next few years. In 1815 she was in France, and travelled to Waterloo to visit the battlefield. Wales was no longer a draw for her, and she engaged to work as maid to a ship's captain. In this position she was able to visit the Americas, Africa

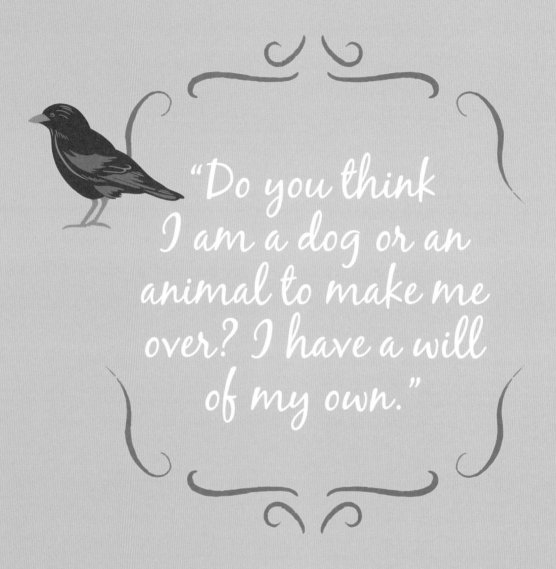

"Do you think I am a dog or an animal to make me over? I have a will of my own."

BETSI CADWALADR
RESPONDS TO FLORENCE NIGHTINGALE'S DEMANDS
THAT SHE BE 'MADE OVER' TO ANOTHER SUPERINTENDENT
1854

and Australia. She was apparently an asset on the ship, drawing on a love of the theatre developed during her time in London to offer impromptu performances. She also took her turn nursing the sick and performing tasks such as assisting in childbirth, despite having no medical training.

When Betsi returned to Britain, she decided to deal with her lack of knowledge, and underwent nurse's training at Guy's Hospital in London. She was no longer young but, undaunted, joined the military nursing service at the age of sixty-five with the intention of travelling to the Crimea. Florence Nightingale was prominent among organisers and trainers of nurses for this conflict, and was strongly of the opinion that Betsi should not go – Betsi was scathing in her response to Nightingale's suggestion that she be 'made over' to another superintendent in the event she did get her way. Nightingale and Betsi belonged to very different social classes, and there is more than a suggestion of snobbery and/or anti-Welsh sentiment in Nightingale's attitude towards Betsi.

Florence Nightingale did not get her wish; Betsi was posted to a Turkish hospital run by Nightingale. The two women clashed regularly, until Betsi decided to leave the hospital for a post closer to the front line. She was a formidable force in this dangerous location, fighting to ensure efficient movement of supplies, and good quality medical care, food and sanitation. Even Nightingale was forced to swallow her dislike of Betsi and acknowledge her achievements.

Conditions in the Crimea were hard, and Betsi did not see out the war at her posting. When she returned to London in 1855 she was ill with cholera and dysentery. She went to live with her sister, where she began work on her autobiography. She lived another five years, dying in 1860. She was buried in a pauper's grave in London.

While the achievements of Florence Nightingale, Mary Seacole and other early nurse pioneers were widely celebrated, Betsi's legacy was neglected for some one hundred and fifty years after her death. Only in the early 2000s did the Royal College of Nursing in Wales recognise the importance of honouring their own badass nurse heroine of the Crimea. A biennial lecture was established in Betsi's honour, and a health board in North Wales named for her. She is now a regular feature on lists of influential Welsh women, and her grave is marked by a new memorial stone to honour her life.

LIVE YOUR LIFE BY BETSI

Betsi was her own woman, and never married despite – by her own account – receiving over twenty proposals of marriage in her lifetime. It is tempting to wonder what made her abandon that first position in Wales – while a life in service is not an appealing one to the modern eye, on paper at least, Betsi's posting seems a good one. Not all servants had leisure time, and still fewer had music tuition to fill it. She would not, of course, be the first servant to flee unwanted sexual advances, and her dramatic escape by means of the old tied-together sheets might suggest such a reading. Certainly she made it clear that another, later flight from Wales was motivated by a desire to avoid marriage.

Instead of marriage, Betsi had fun, fulfilment in her career, and a chance to see the world. Make like Betsi and learn to like your own company. What seems a negative when called 'loneliness' seems much more of a positive when framed as 'solitude', 'privacy' or 'me-time'. Use time alone to reflect on what you want, and what you might need to do to get there. Then you can focus on putting in place anything you might need to help you fulfil your goals.

LADY
CHARLOTTE GUEST
TRANSLATOR

When Lady Charlotte Elizabeth Bertie was born to Albermarle Bertie, 9th Earl of Lindsey and his second wife Charlotte in 1812, few in her family's circle could have anticipated the young aristocrat's future role in cementing a cornerstone of Welsh cultural identity. Young Charlotte's life looked set to be one of exceptional privilege, but the reality was rather different. Her father died when she was six years old, and in the same year she narrowly escaped a house fire. Her mother remarried to a clergyman Charlotte did not like, and after a brood of half-siblings were born, her mother's health began to fail. Charlotte inherited her duties in the running of the home, but happily she benefitted from an acute mind and apparently limitless reserves of energy. She had a particular interest in politics and an aptitude for languages; through self-study and access to her brothers' tutor she learned Arabic, Hebrew and Persian, Latin, Greek, French and Italian. While it scarcely seems possible that she had any time for leisure, she did learn the skills considered appropriate for a lady of her class, such as dancing and music.

To their credit, Charlotte's suitors appear to have been attracted more by the strength of her mind and her political convictions than by her elegant dance steps. One early suitor was Benjamin Disraeli, who would go on to serve twice as prime minister of the United Kingdom. At the age of twenty-one, Charlotte went to London, where she met John Josiah Guest. Guest owned Dowlais Ironworks in Wales – the largest ironworks of the time – and had been elected Member of

"The idea appeared
to me so absurd that
I rebelled outright and
insisted upon using the
wooden mallet, to the
no small amusement
of the workmen."

CHARLOTTE GUEST REFUSES AN ORNAMENTAL HAMMER
TO LAY THE FIRST STONE OF THE TAFF VALE RAILWAY
1837

Parliament for Merthyr Tydfil. He was considerably Charlotte's senior at forty-nine, but the marriage was apparently a success and ten children followed (Charlotte seems to have done nothing by halves). Despite some issues relating to the difference in their standing – Guest was wealthy but considered socially inferior to his wife – Charlotte was able to engage in philanthropic activities designed to improve the conditions of the workers at Dowlais. Informed by the working-class Chartism movement, she saw the value in developing educational and leisure provision, supporting schools and a library, and with 'Merthyr' (she called her husband after his constituency) she also worked to improve sanitation by such means as piping clean water into houses.

Charlotte's interests in leisure and languages combined in her activities during this period as a patron of the arts and particularly as a scholar, translator and promoter of Welsh literature. By 1837 she had learned Welsh, established a network of literary scholars, and begun an edition and translation of *The Mabinogion* – a series of Middle Welsh stories preserved in various manuscript sources. The first part was published in 1838 with a further six parts following by 1845. She published a three-volume edition in 1846 and a revised edition in 1877. Her work stood as the standard edition until 1948 and is still read today. Its influence in promoting awareness of Welsh literature, language and culture was enormous, and it has played a significant part in influencing writers from Tennyson to Tolkein.

Charlotte supported Guest in running the ironworks and took a greater load as Guest's health declined. When he died in 1852, she ran the business until she could pass it on to her son. She married again, to a classical scholar fourteen years her junior. He became a Member of Parliament with her support, and during their marriage and extensive travels Charlotte amassed important collections of china and other artefacts, which she bequeathed to the Victoria and Albert and British Museums. She outlived her second husband, dying at the grand old age of eighty-two.

A NOTE

In her translation, Charlotte used the title *Mabinogion* – in fact, the four 'branches' of story are the *Mabinogi*. 'Mabinogion' appears once in a manuscript source, and Charlotte may have understood this as a plural of 'Mabinogi'; it is more likely, however, that this was a transcription error. Charlotte's book contains other stories from manuscript sources, and today a distinction is made between the *Mabinogi* – the four branches – and the *Mabinogion*, the bigger collection.

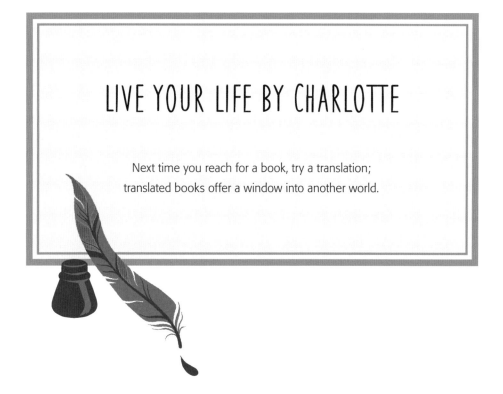

LIVE YOUR LIFE BY CHARLOTTE

Next time you reach for a book, try a translation;
translated books offer a window into another world.

'REBECCA'
AND
JANE WALTERS
PROTESTOR AND COUNTER~PROTESTOR

O n 13 May 1839, under cover of darkness, *Merched Beca* or 'Rebecca' and her 'daughters' descended on Yr Efail Wen, on the border between Pembrokeshire and Carmarthenshire. Their object was a tollgate; before they were done with it, it was utterly demolished. Another gate was erected in the same place, but within a month 'Rebecca' and some three or four hundred of her 'daughters' had torn that one down too. The local Turnpike Trust gave in; Yr Efail Wen's tollgate would not be re-erected.

This was the first of Wales's 'Rebecca' riots. But the furious figures in women's clothing, their faces blackened with soot, were not, in fact, women at all – or at least, not in the main. They were men in women's attire, symbolically invoking the Bible verse that says of Rebecca, 'Thou art our sister; be thou the mother of thousands of millions, and let thy seed possess the gates of those which hate them.' The farmers of Wales had a big issue with gates – specifically the tollgates set up across the country to raise monies to pay for the upkeep of the roads. The trusts that had set these up were not well regulated, and unscrupulous profiteering was rampant. A farmer going to market or collecting lime to fertilise his fields might have to pass through multiple tollgates to get to his destination and home again, seriously impacting on his ability to survive in an already-hostile climate of failing harvests, high rents and taxes.

The tollgates were not the only injustice suffered by the local populace, but they were a tangible and – importantly – ill-defended symbol to attack. After their "the threatening letters which they receive reminds them that their lives, their families and their property is in danger every moment"

JANE WATERS DESCRIBES INTIMIDATION OF LANDOWNERS DURING THE REBECCA RIOTS IN A LETTER TO THE HOME OFFICE 1843 victory at Yr Efail Wen, 'Rebecca' and her 'daughters' were quiet for a time, but in the summer of 1843 they rose again. This time they had their eye more broadly on the landlord classes. Nocturnal acts of arson and vandalism aimed at inducing reductions in rents were reported in the press and became the talk of Britain.

At this point, 'Rebecca' took on a woman who did not intend to yield.

Jane Walters was the youngest child of a prosperous family of farmers from Perthcereint in Cardiganshire. After Jane's mother's death she, her father and her two sisters had relocated to a fine house outside Newcastle Emlyn. It was called Glanmedeni.

The Walters family lived a comfortable life. The girls were educated in boarding schools and attended balls and parties at home in Cardigan, and in fashionable bathing towns such as Aberystwyth. Despite this social whirl Jane did not marry and she and her sister Frances remained at home, continuing to live at Glanmedeni after their father died. Jane was a Methodist involved in good works in the local area and a keen supporter of the Welsh language. But still she attracted the attention of 'Rebecca' and her 'daughters'.

The first issue with which the rioters were concerned was historic; they believed that Jane's father had defaulted on a payment owed to a servant, Dina Davies, some twenty years before. 'Rebecca' wrote to Jane threatening a visit unless Jane and Frances paid the debt of £1 plus interest. The second issue also concerned an incident that had taken place some years before. Around 1838 a group of revellers leaving a wedding near Cardigan had passed Jane and Frances. One young man was dared to kiss one of the sisters. He kissed Jane, winning himself half a crown, but was later fined £1 for his misconduct.

Motivated by these grievances, 'Rebecca' descended on Glanmedeni on the evening of 4 September 1843. As the rioters pounded on the door, capturing the male outdoor servants, Jane, Frances and their maid reatreated upstairs, where Jane opened a window and addressed the rioters in Welsh. She reminded them of the good work she and her sister had done and pleaded with them to be reasonable.

'We have very great respect for you,' one of the protesters cried out, 'but money we must and will have.'

Shots were fired, a window was broken and various small acts of vandalism were carried out in the grounds. Chillingly, a length of rope tied into a noose was left near the house as a warning. Jane and Frances took the threat seriously, moving to a house in Newcastle Emlyn and employing guards to keep watch on Glanmedeni. Jane took up their case with the Home Office in a series of letters detailing their situation and the events of the attack on Glanmedeni. In the letters – which are now in the National Archives in London – Jane reveals that she believed the majority of the rioters to be disaffected youths suffering poor treatment by their landlords and employers, egged on by a small number of outside elements seeking to manipulate the local lads to achieve their own ends. She believed that these people or persons were responsible for the letters signed by 'Rebecca'. This desire to believe in outside interference might be read kindly as an implicit trust in Welsh people – Jane was, after all, Welsh herself and a lover of the country and its culture – or as a landowner's rather patronising failure to credit locals with the ability to organise effectively.

In her letters Jane criticised those charged with enforcing the law in Wales for a lax attitude to the original riots, and for being out of touch with the local people, as evidenced by the fact that many magistrates could not understand Welsh, the first and only language of many of the local population. She believed that she had a firmer understanding of the country, and an insight into the trials the people had suffered.

Jane and Frances offered a reward for information on the Glanmedeni attack. It was initially set at £50, and eventually raised to £500, but no information was forthcoming to set the sisters' minds at rest. Later Jane offered the Home Office land on which to build barracks to house soldiers. By this time the riots had largely ceased, in part due to increased army presence in the region, and in part because most rioters had no wish to engage in violence beyond the destruction of tollgates and relatively minor damage to property to draw attention to their protests.

Jane and Frances lived at Newcastle Emlyn until Frances died in 1851. Jane returned to Glanmedeni, living out the rest of her life there until her death in 1881 at the age of eighty-eight. She had fought back in her own way. 'Rebecca' had not cost her her home, or her love of Wales, its language and its people.

Meanwhile, 'Rebecca' had her own victory, in a sense. Some rents reduced, toll rates were improved, and eventually the Turnpikes, South Wales Act 1844 simplified and reduced the system. The idea of a collective uprising had a strong effect on Welsh society, and peaceful protest has been a feature of Welsh politics ever since.

LIVE YOUR LIFE BY 'REBECCA'

Protest – peaceful, violent or in complex combinations of the two – functions to raise awareness. There is real danger that when the media cycle moves on, change does not happen. Don't let this happen to the Black Lives Matter protests. We need change at all levels of society. From investment in mental health services and youth work to better social housing, building a fairer society helps those facing structural barriers, who are first to bear the brunt of flawed systems. You can help keep these issues on the political radar through continuing action, engagement with your MP, MSP or TD, and support for campaigning organisations.

"lying on her bed, decorated as a bride, having round her head a wreath of flowers"

SARAH 'SAL' JACOB
VICTIM OF MANSLAUGHTER

Sarah Jacob, known to her family as 'Sal', was born in May 1857 to Hannah and Evan Jacob on the farm they rented near the village of Llanfihangel-ar-Arth in Carmarthenshire. She was one of six children brought up in this Welsh-speaking household. Hannah and Evan were respectable, hard-working folk with strong religious belief.

In February 1867, when Sarah was nine years old, she took to her bed with an unknown ailment that began with stomach pain and escalated to cause convulsions and loss of consciousness. She was seriously ill for months, only fully regaining consciousness in May, by which time handfuls of her long dark hair had fallen out and she was skeletally thin. The family began to build her strength up with milk, rice, porridge and fruit. As she convalesced she was allowed to remain in her parents' bedroom, a rather warmer and more comfortable place than the loft she normally shared with her siblings. She was of course excused her share of the farm work, and instead spent her days in reading the Bible and composing poems as her strength returned.

Perhaps Sarah was loath to allow this cosseting to come to an end, because by autumn of that year her recovery had been interrupted by a refusal to accept any food whatsoever. In this behaviour she joined a small group of Victorian 'Fasting Girls', mostly pubescent girls who claimed to be able to survive over indefinite periods of time without food or other nourishment beyond the spiritual. Most of these girls claimed to derive their miraculous ability from a higher power, in the manner of saints of the Middle Ages such as Catherine of

Siena. While Sarah was certainly religious, it is not clear whether her refusal to eat was initially motivated by her spiritual beliefs. The extent of her parents' collusion is also difficult to determine. They certainly professed to believe that she was not eating; they later swore that no food had passed Sarah's lips after 10 October 1867, when she was ten years old.

As Sarah's fasting continued, she became something of a local celebrity. The second half of the nineteenth century was a time of rapid development of scientific thought, which threatened traditional adherence to religion. In her deeply spiritual and conservative community, Sarah was a phenomenon precisely because her 'miracle' could not be explained by medical science.

The local vicar was a fervent believer in Sarah's powers, and he took it upon himself to spread the word far and wide. He wrote to the press of the 'Welsh Fasting Girl', and Sarah became an overnight sensation. Spectators thronged to the farm from across England and Wales, walking miles from the station at Pencader to gaze in wonder at Sarah as she lay in bed surrounded by flowers, with her Bible and her poetic compositions in hand. She looked the picture of health, with her long hair grown back and her adult teeth come in. Her visitors left gifts and money on the bed, or on their way out of the house. 'Her eyes shone like pearls,' one visitor remarked. 'She had rosy cheeks and looked like a lily amongst thorns.'

A backlash quickly began against Sarah's claims in the press and particularly in medical journals. In the spring of 1869 Sarah underwent a test in which a local committee watched her to ensure she was receiving no sustenance. This was not a particularly stringent process, given the potential for local bias and the facts both that Sarah's sister was allowed to sleep with her and the committee was not allowed to inspect her bedclothes. Unsurprisingly, the committee found her claims to be true.

In November of 1869, a more thorough watch was proposed. This time a 'Watchers' Committee' of medical staff from Guy's Hospital in London would watch Sarah round the clock. Evan and Hannah agreed, apparently keen to have their belief vindicated. The circumstances of the watch seem unbelievable to a modern eye; since the aim was to catch Sarah out in her suspected fraud, these trained nurses did nothing to aid her but instead mounted a 24-hour watch while the twelve-year-old child starved to death. They were instructed to feed her only if she asked. She did not ask; to do so would be to admit having lied, to herself or others. It seems that by the end the committee had thought the better of it and wished to call off the watch, but Sarah's parents would not allow it.

One might say that Sarah was dying to prove herself, and die she did, after more than eight days without food or water. If she had previously crept out of bed at night to consume small morsels of food, or been surreptitiously fed by her siblings via kisses – a trick used by other famous 'Fasting Girls' – she no longer had recourse to such help. Under the eye of the committee, she lapsed into unconsciousness five days after the watch began, and died of starvation on 17 December 1869.

A post-mortem found that Sarah had bones from a small animal or fish in her stomach, and faeces further down in her intestines, indicating that – of course – she had consumed at least small amounts of food prior to the last watch. An inquest found that she had died of negligence and both Hannah and Evan Jacob were tried and convicted of manslaughter. Evan was sentenced to a year's hard labour, and Hannah to six months. No member of the committee paid for their part in Sarah's death; they were protected from prosecution by prior agreement.

What motivated Evan and Hannah Jacob? A sceptic might say the money, but well over a year passed before Sarah's fame spread beyond their immediate community and began to attract gifts. They might have manipulated her owing to their own religious beliefs or a desire for attention, but equally she might have manipulated them for similar reasons of her own. Many modern commentators believe that she was suffering from a form of anorexia, an eating disorder and mental illness characterised by self-destructive behaviour and often by the manipulation of others as a complex expression of emotions.

There is a distinctly anti-Welsh slant to much of the contemporary coverage of the Jacob trial, and a shocking lack of attention to the cruelty of what was ultimately an abusive medical experiment perpetrated on a child of twelve. *The Lancet* later noted the disgraceful conduct of the medical professionals in the case, writing that medical practitioners everywhere should be 'filled with feelings of shame and indignation' as a result.

LIVE YOUR LIFE BY SARAH

Sarah may well have had undiagnosed anorexia. Understanding of eating disorders was in its infancy during her era, but the medical professionals dealing with her case appear to have been far less interested in pursuing medical answers than by uncovering fraud in a working-class, religious Welsh family. This has had disturbing echoes through the decades, for example when flawed statistical evidence presented in court by Professor Sir Roy Meadow in 1999 resulted in solicitor Sally Clark being found guilty of murdering her two baby sons, both of whom had actually died of natural causes. When Clark's conviction was finally overturned, two further women's convictions and another ongoing case were also recognised as miscarriages of justice.

These cases are (thankfully) extreme and rare; on the other hand, studies regularly show that women are more likely to wait longer for a health diagnosis and to be misdiagnosed with a mental health problem. Sex is key to a 'health gap' seen in medical systems in all countries in the world. Male-default thinking sees male presentation of illness deemed 'classic' and female presentations 'non-standard'. Medical research does not adequately provide for the physical differences between women and men. Reproductive and 'hormonal' issues become a catch-all misdiagnosis for anything from colon cancer to brain tumours. Race, class, weight, sexual orientation and trans status all affect clinical care as well, leaving many women navigating multiple, intersecting prejudices.

It is very difficult to know how to tackle a pervasive issue like implicit bias. Take notes with you to medical appointments, to help you structure a conversation and ensure you receive answers. Don't be afraid to ask for

LIVE YOUR LIFE BY SARAH

a further referral if you remain concerned. If you are worried about how you are being or might be spoken to, take someone with you to medical appointments to support you. Depressingly, some women have found that a male partner or friend vouching for their pain or other symptoms is taken more seriously than they are.

"Always keep a 'Jif' in the house. It will save many an hour of pain."

MARKETING SLOGAN FOR SARAH MORGAN~JONES'S
PHARMACEUTICAL PREPARATION

SARAH
MORGAN-JONES
ENTREPRENEUR

I f you'd picked up a Welsh news-sheet such as the snappily titled *Haverfordwest and Milford Haven Telegraph and General Weekly Reporter* in the early years of the twentieth century, you would have been beset with a bewildering array of must-have products on the advertising pages. No mother should let her child be without 'Harrison's Pomade', a sure and certain remedy against nits and lice. 'Royal Windsor' corsets guaranteed the perfect shape for that elegant, slim-skirted look that was so in vogue. Fred Lloyd the Builders were also doing funerals; handy, one imagines, if the turn for the coffin was tight on the stairs. Other products and offerings included rat poison guaranteed to dry out rats' bodies with no smell, 'Arabian Oil Embrocation' for farm animals, and for those suffering from headache, toothache or other pain, there were *really affordable* hard narcotics.

Pharmacist John Morgan-Jones's advert guaranteed that 'Jif' powders would shift any aches and pains double-quick for a mere tuppence each, or a shilling the dozen. The powders were manufactured by his enterprising wife Sarah in their pharmacy in Carmarthen, and they probably did work to relieve pain. Unfortunately they were also highly addictive, as John found out to his cost.

Sarah was born Sarah Jones in Carmarthenshire, the daughter of David Jones and his second wife, also Sarah. She married John in 1899. Back then he was plain Jones, too, but he found 'John Jones' a less than useful name when travelling – his father was possessed of the rather amazing first name 'Sylvanus' and so presumably didn't have the same problem. At home John went by the nickname 'Jack Syl' (i.e. Sylvanus's son Jack), but that wouldn't do in his business as a pharmacist and herbalist. Sarah, too, had a mind for marketing and saw the benefit of standing out among all of Wales's Morgans and Joneses by combining the two names. Morgan had been John's mother's maiden name, and the maiden name, too, of Sarah's father's first wife.

If the Morgan-Joneses' aim was to attract a better class of customer for their now grander-sounding business, they certainly succeeded. At the height of their popularity, 'Jif' powders acquired devotees across the globe and in the highest echelons of society, including the Tsar of Russia and the Kaiser in Germany. From this distance it's hard to say whether the appeal was pain relief or a genteel means of achieving a nice little high.

The powders, like many pharmaceutical preparations of their era, contained opiates. Before the Drug Enforcement Act of 1920 tackled widespread availability of opium and its derivatives, Sarah was fully at liberty to sell her powders across the counter and by mail order to all comers. By the time of the Act, opiate addiction was a widespread problem in society, but still there was a common argument that individuals chose to use opiates for pain relief at their own risk, understanding the potential issues. To a modern eye, the 'Jif' powders adverts make no mention of the possible dangers of the preparation – advertising was also unregulated, and would remain so for some decades.

John and Sarah's marriage collapsed under the pressure of his addiction and they were separated by 1903, when John died in St Pancras Hospital in London. This was the infirmary of a large workhouse; despite Sarah's best efforts, John died a ruined man. Understanding of addiction was in its infancy and it is likely that he received little or no useful support by the standards of today.

After John's death, Sarah remarried. The dealer in legal opiates chose for her second husband a clergyman, one Thomas Thomas. He was rather sweetly known as 'Tommy Twice' and was a steady influence in the life of Sarah and John's son, David Sylvanus Morgan-Jones. He followed in his mother's footsteps – in a sense – by training as a doctor.

LIVE YOUR LIFE BY SARAH

Today Sarah's story is remembered only by her family; this, of course, is the case for most lives and almost always for women's lives. Sarah bequeathed a more comfortable life to her children, and their children, than she had herself, and while her methods may seem a little dubious today, she operated within the legal framework of her time and her hard work should not be denied.

Remember the stories of your female forebears and share them with your sons and daughters, nephews and nieces. Whether your great-great-granny worked in a mill or wore fine clothes on her back, cleaned a great house or lived in one, was 'respectable' or uproarious, she was a survivor in a time when women had few rights and fewer protections, particularly against the greatest danger they faced in life, in the form of childbirth.

Sarah Morgan-Jones was my husband's great-grandmother. In this spirit of remembering, she is featured in this book.

"prejudice and a fear of
competition underlay a
good deal of the opposition
shown to women wishing to
enter the legal profession"

ASCRIBED TO GWYNETH BEBB
SPEAKING AT A DINNER
1913

GWYNETH MARJORIE BEBB

CAMPAIGNER

When Gwyneth Marjorie Bebb brought an action against the Law Society in 1913, seeking the right to practise as a lawyer, she was challenging accepted wisdom reaching back as far as the fourteenth century. 'Fems ne poient estre attorneyes,' law textbook *The Mirror of Justices* asserts. 'Women may not be attorneys.'

Gwyneth Bebb was born in 1889 to Llewellyn and Louisa Bebb (neé Traer) and moved to Wales at the age of nine, when her father was appointed Principal of St David's College in Lampeter. She studied Jurisprudence at St Hugh's College, Oxford, and achieved a first in her exams, but she could not be awarded a degree due to her sex and so did not graduate. In 1913 she and three other women – Karin Costelloe, Maud Ingram and Frances Nettlefold – applied to the Law Society to sit the preliminary examinations that would allow them to become articled clerks and, ultimately, solicitors. They included the requisite fee with their applications. The Law Society returned these monies, advising that no woman presenting for examination would be permitted to proceed, since no woman could be admitted as a solicitor. So far, so fourteenth century.

Gwyneth and the others chose to bring an action against the society, which became known as *Bebb v. Law Society*. Gwyneth sought a declaration that she was a 'person' within the meaning of the Solicitors Act 1843, which stated, 'No person shall act as an Attorney or Solicitor [. . .] unless such Person shall after the passing of this Act be admitted and enrolled and otherwise duly qualified as an Attorney or Solicitor, pursuant to the Directions and Regulations of this Act.' It also stated that 'every word importing the Masculine Gender only shall extend and be applied to a Female as well as Male [. . .] unless in any of the Cases aforesaid it be otherwise specially provided, or there by something in the Subject or Context, repugnant to such Construction'.

The High Court appears to have found the radical suggestion that women were people for the purposes of statute 'repugnant'; Gwyneth's case was dismissed. Undaunted, Gwyneth went to the Court of Appeal, where her case was heard in December 1913. Her Counsel, Lord Robert Cecil KC, argued that women had a right to be admitted unless there had been an absolute rule of law to disqualify them; he submitted that there was no such statute. He noted several arguments to the contrary: women had acted as 'attorneys' for their husbands in the reign of King Edward III; women were permitted to practise as solicitors overseas; the recent trend of legislation had been to open opportunities to women. 'There is no reason in the nature of things why women should not practise,' he said, 'and the plaintiff is a particularly capable person.'

A lawyer once said that lawyers don't deal in justice, they deal in the law, and the 'justices' hearing the appeal disagreed with Robert Cecil that the statute could be interpreted to include women. They concluded that the Act was passed in a context of 'long uniform and uninterrupted usage' of women being disqualified from being solicitors; therefore there was a principle established at common law that a women could not be a solicitor. The courts could not change this; it was a matter for parliament. The *Mirror of Justices* was cited, and it was noted that married women were even more 'unfitted either for entering into articles or for contracting with their clients', because they were not at absolute liberty to enter into binding contracts. Imagine if a woman became a solicitor and then inconvenienced her clients by getting married half way through a case and becoming even more unable to do the job!

Despite the failure of her case, Gwyneth received largely favourable press coverage, with the *Express* writing, '[i]f a woman can take a first class in law at Oxford, what right has the Law Society to prevent her from earning her living as a solicitor?'

Gwyneth continued to engage with political action and feminist activism, seeing the combination as key to achieving her aims as momentum grew for legislative change, despite the best efforts of the Law Society. She married a solicitor, moved from the Board of Trade to the Ministry of Food, and gave birth to her first daughter, Diana.

In 1918 the Bar in England and Wales voted 178 to 22 against admitting women at its Annual General Meeting. But events had overtaken them and their hand was forced when, in 1919, the Sex Disqualification (Removal) Act was passed, allowing women to be lawyers. Gwyneth applied to join Lincoln's Inn as a student barrister – on a previous occasion she had of course been refused – and was admitted in January 1920, shortly after Diana's birth. She continued with her studies through a second pregnancy, but complications saw both Gwyneth and her prematurely born child die in 1921. She did not achieve the career in law she sought for herself, but her determination paved the way for countless other women to realise their legal ambitions.

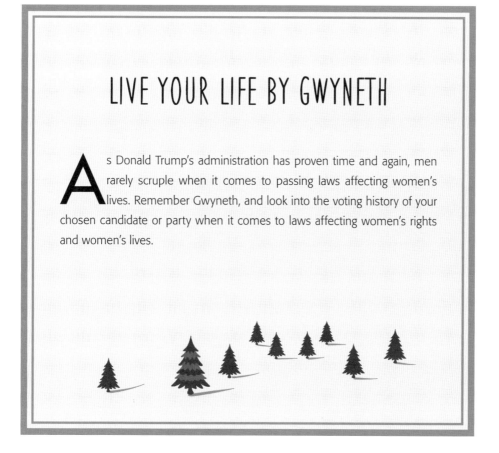

LIVE YOUR LIFE BY GWYNETH

As Donald Trump's administration has proven time and again, men rarely scruple when it comes to passing laws affecting women's lives. Remember Gwyneth, and look into the voting history of your chosen candidate or party when it comes to laws affecting women's rights and women's lives.

"The trouble with feminists is that they put themselves on an equal with men. Well I'm a woman and I'm much stronger than any man."

LAURA ASHLEY'S WORDS AS RECALLED BY HER SON DAVID
ON THE THIRTIETH ANNIVERSARY OF HER DEATH IN 2015

LAURA ASHLEY
FASHION DESIGNER AND ENTREPRENEUR

Think of Laura Ashley's fabric, fashion and furniture designs and you aren't likely to conjure up any sort of visual embodiment of 'Wales' or 'badass'. Instead you might imagine a vision of classic English style. This belies the fact that their creator was born, raised and worked in Wales, and was a most determined and savvy woman.

Laura Mountney's parents were Welsh but living in London, where her father was in the civil service. They were keen that any children should be born in Wales, and so Laura made her entrance at 31 Station Road, Dowlais, Merthyr Tydfil on 7 September 1925, in her grandmother's home. The family were Strict Baptists and young Laura attended Welsh language services although she could not speak the language. She attended Marshall's school in Merthyr Tydfil and then Elmwood school in Croydon. When war broke out, she was evacuated back to Wales.

After school Laura served in the 'Wrens' – the Women's Royal Naval Service. She was a fan of the uniform, recalling the style in its 'nice, cheeky little hat' and good quality cloth. While in the Wrens she met Bernard Ashley, a young engineer. They began a courtship which lasted the course even when Bernard was posted to India after the war. They married in 1949 and moved into a flat in Pimlico in London, where Laura combined work as a secretary for the National Federation of Women's Institutes with care of their first two children.

The Women's Institute promoted traditional craft skills such as quilting, which Laura had enjoyed as a younger woman with her grandmother in Wales.

Seeking pretty fabrics for use in her quilts, she discovered that the small, ditsy floral prints of the Victorian era she preferred were no longer available to buy. She and Bernard – who had an interest in colour and design as well as engineering skills – invested their savings in a screenprint set-up, dyes and linen, and began designing and producing printed fabric for headscarves, napkins, table linens and tea-towels. Laura focused on design and Bernard printed the fabrics in a small production line in their home.

The Ashleys sold their scarves by mail order and through high street suppliers including John Lewis. Bernard left his job in the City to dedicate his time to 'Ashley Mountney' as they called their company. It was eventually renamed 'Laura Ashley' on Bernard's initiative, as he thought the more feminine name would appeal to their target customer.

In the early days the start-up pushed the Ashleys almost to breaking point. Margins were tight, working capital scarce, and all profits were reinvested into the business. In 1955 Bernard and Laura moved operations to a cottage in Kent, where the family (now six) lived and worked, and came close to disaster when the River Darent burst its banks, flooding the premises. In 1960 Laura packed up the children and set up camp – literally – on the banks of Mawddach Estuary near Dolgellau. In 1961 the Ashleys opened a shop on Maengwyn Street in Machynlleth in 1961, selling their products with a small range of locally produced goods such as honey and living in the accommodation above. Laura began to develop the line to include clothing, working with local seamstresses to create loose shirts and gardening smocks. As the business grew, the family moved again, to Carno in Powys, where they first took over an empty social club, and later the disused railway station. While Carno would remain the headquarters, eventually they would open factories across north and mid Wales to cope with demand. Former staff testify that they were popular employers, if slightly odd in terms of their 'hippy' attitudes to life in what was still a very traditional place. Laura's son recalls that his mother, 'was 100 per cent into workers' rights. My mother's politics stemmed from her attitude as a manager of a business and that the chain is only as strong as the weakest link. So the weakest link is the person you have to take care of the most'.

The first major boutique opened in Pelham Street, South Kensington, in 1968, truly launching Laura Ashley onto the fashion scene. From there, Laura's dresses came to define a generation. Viewed by many commentators as a reaction to the short, tight fashions of the 1960s, the 'Laura Ashley Look' offered Victorian-style frocks in flowered cottons, with full skirts and sleeves and high necks, softened with lace trims and embellishments. Floppy felt hats brought the look up-to-date for the 1970s.

By the 1980s, the Ashley empire included 220 shops worldwide, and some 5,000 outlets carried the line. The company had received an especial boost when Charles, Prince of Wales married Lady Diana Spencer, who was a fan of the brand. When 'Lady Di' was pictured in one particular Laura Ashley blouse, demand became so great that production eventually had to be shut down. The look appealed as much to women in the 1980s as their mothers and sisters in the 1970s; in the era of power dressing and shoulder pads, it projected an air of countryside charm. The Ashleys retained family control of the business, with all of Laura's children involved. The family amassed enormous wealth, acquiring a yacht, a private plane, a French chateau and a villa in the Bahamas.

Sadly, Laura did not enjoy her success into old age. She died in 1985 at just sixty, of a cerebral hemhorrage after a fall at her daughter's house. She was buried in Wales, at Carno. Two months later, Bernard floated the company on the stock market. The enterprise begun on the Ashleys' kitchen table was valued at around £200 million.

In the years since, the Laura Ashley brand has struggled to regain the highs of the 1970s and 1980s. The move to clean-lined Scandinavian style in the home hit particularly hard, and the 1990s saw tough trading and a series of relaunches followed by a bailout. It does, however, remain a world-famous brand and the Laura Ashley look comes round again and again in the hands of other designers. The 2019 iteration was even ascribed to a reaction against the bodycon look of the Kardashians; Laura might have approved.

LIVE YOUR LIFE BY LAURA

There is much to inspire in Laura's life, from the determination that saw her learn to screenprint from a library book, to the work ethic that kept her going through the tough times to achieve worldwide success. In today's world, there is perhaps also inspiration in her attitude towards waste. 'I don't like ephemeral things;' she said, 'I like things that last forever', and 'people should hang on to the things they like. They don't need closets full of clothes.'

Laura's clothes and other goods were solid, locally made, generally utilised natural fibres and safe dyes and still turn up in the vintage trade today, entirely wearable after fifty years. Compare the fast-fashion of the modern world, clogging landfill after only a couple of wears.

Live life by Laura, and seek out vintage and sustainable clothing, and items that will go the distance. If you won't wear it at least thirty times, step away. If a once-on outfit is what you really, really want for a special event, head down to your local charity shop or vintage dealer – you can guarantee no one will turn up in the same outfit and you can sell it or donate it again after you have worn it. Even a wedding dress (I can attest!) might be found on Gumtree or in your mother's wardrobe . . .

BETTY CAMPBELL
HEADTEACHER

Wales, in common with Scotland and Ireland, has few statues and other public memorials to its women. In early 2019 a public vote was held to select a woman from Welsh history to be immortalised in a statue in Central Square in Cardiff. The women nominated were poet, writer and master mariner Sarah Jane Rees ('Cranogwen'), suffragette Margaret Haig Mackworth, Labour Party stalwart Elizabeth Andrews, writer and anthropologist Elaine Morgan, and Betty Campbell.

Betty was born Jane Elizabeth Johnston in Butetown in Cardiff in 1934 and brought up in the multi-ethnic community of Tiger Bay, the city's dockland district. Her father was killed in the Second World War and Betty's mother struggled to keep body and soul together.

Betty was a born reader, adoring the school stories of Enid Blyton in particular. These reflected her own academic ambitions, which she seemed close to realising when she won a scholarship to Cardiff's Lady Margaret High School for Girls. Betty was a match for her better-off classmates in academic terms, but she soon discovered that she did not meet them on an equal playing field. Betty was Black, and when she told the headteacher she would like to follow in her footsteps and train to teach, she was told that, 'My dear, the problems would be insurmountable.'

Later Betty recalled returning to her desk in tears, but the knock-back did not deter her. She had her sights firmly set on teaching – a very popular career

"In our own unique way we were establishing an area where religion and colour didn't matter – we all respected each other as people."

BETTY CAMPBELL ON BUTETOWN

choice of Welsh women of her generation – and she persevered. She became one of only six women in the first intake of female students to Cardiff Teacher Training College in 1960. She was by then a wife and a mother, but she successfully juggled these family commitments with her training and qualified as a teacher.

Betty's first job was in Llanrumney, but soon she was back in her own birthplace of Butetown, where again she faced racism, this time from parents who were not convinced that a Black teacher could be as good as a white one. Betty proved them wrong, teaching in Butetown for twenty-eight years and rising through the ranks to be headteacher of her own school – and Wales' first Black headteacher.

Betty's pioneering spirit did not stop there. She had made a trip to the USA and been inspired by the story of former slave and abolitionist Harriet Tubman, and by other key figures in the Civil Rights movement. Following in their example, she decided to put Black culture on the curriculum in her school. 'I was determined that I was going to become one of those people,' she told the Welsh Assembly, 'and enhance the Black spirit, Black culture as much as I could.' As part of her work to promote understanding of the contribution made to life in Britain by people of colour, Betty helped to establish Black History Month, an annual celebration of the contribution of people of African and Carribean descent to all our lives.

Betty's work took her further into public life, joining the UK Home Office's race advisory committee and becoming a member of the Commission for Racial Equality. She also served as a councillor for Butetown, a board member of BBC Wales and was awarded an MBE for services to education and community. She was invited to meet Nelson Mandela when he was presented with the freedom of the city of Cardiff.

Betty died in 2017, but her memory will be cemented for generations when her statue is raised in Central Square: she was elected Wales' public choice for their 'Hidden Heroine' most worthy of commemoration.

LIVE YOUR LIFE BY BETTY

Betty faced racism for much of her life. Don't fall into the trap of believing that racism doesn't exist any more. Unconcious bias affects personal and professional interactions across society and its effects are pervasive. Be open to your own biases and take action to address these in terms of how you interact with others. Aim to focus on fair treatment and respect for others at all times.

CONCLUDING WORDS
A WOMAN'S WORK IS NEVER DONE

This book does not aim to be exhaustive in any way. The women portrayed here do not represent all the women of Scotland, of Ireland, or of Wales. They do not represent their eras, their cultures, their faiths or their communities. Each story is of an individual who lived her own individual reality, and the strictures of writing short sketches are such that only elements of each life may be included. All were richer than can be reflected here, and that is true even when we know little more than the bare facts related on these pages – or, indeed, less, since some of these stories draw on much less than perfect knowledge. On that note, it must be acknowledged that many of the women would not recognise the sentiments in the sections which seek to find inspiration in their lives. Their times were not our times and their thoughts, values and standards were not ours. They may have viewed their stories very differently; indeed they might not recognise these portraits at all.

It might also be noted that the book, in its focus on inspiring a general reader of today by introducing women of the past, replicates to a degree the wrong that has been done to women by history. It treats them rather in isolation from men, unless their interactions with men were particularly key to a course of action or chain of events. Then, as now, women and men's lives were of course interwoven and hopefully the history of the future will be enriched by a new equality of approach to both sexes.

The book adopts a title designed to catch the eye, but it might also be said to replicate a wrong if, in doing so, it suggests that women must adopt 'male' characteristics to be taken seriously. Both strength and womanhood come in many guises, as their stories amply demonstrate.

The number of women included is, of course, very small and choosing the women was not an easy task. For every Agnes Clerke, Esther Inglis or Gwyneth Bebb included, a Maria Edgeworth, Anna Hume or Frances Hobban was left out. Women's stories are now being uncovered more and more through the good offices of writers, broadcasters, programmers, curators and others. Edinburgh's City Art Centre, for example, staged an exhibition in 2019 of the work of Mary Cameron, an all-but-forgotten contemporary of Phoebe Anna Traquair's who painted bullfights and other work atypical for a woman artist of her time.

Hopefully this work will continue, locally and nationally, drawing on previously unedited manuscripts, family papers and more. Our lives can only be enriched by knowing the stories of those who have gone before us and by channelling their examples. Who wouldn't want to live their life by Catharine Cudney who, in the 1880 Irish census, stated her occupation as 'Does as she pleases'?

TAING ~ BUÍOCHAS ~ DIOLCHAU
THANKS

The manuscript for this book was completed and edited as Covid-19 spread across the globe. In that context of enormous challenge for the book industry (and society as a whole), I am deeply grateful to Ali, Campbell and all at Black & White for continuing to believe in this book and its women's stories. Particular thanks go to Alice and Emma for their careful and insightful attention to the text, to Tonje and Thomas for making it look so very beautiful, and to Laura for her enthusiastic championing of it out in the world. I have to pinch myself to believe that the amazing Helen Crawford-White again created the cover, having made *Warriors and Witches and Damn Rebel Bitches* so very lovely.

Warriors and Witches was greeted with huge generosity by readers, bookshops, festival programmers and audiences across the country. Many of the people I've met while out and about have suggested women for me to write about – not all have made it in here, but I keep a long list and I'm not finished yet. Particular thanks go to my mother-in-law, Liz Morgan-Jones, for introducing me to 'Rebecca' and for sharing my late father-in-law Anthony's notes on his grandmother Sarah's life and line. Thanks to Kirsty MacDonald for pointing me in the direction of Historic Environment Scotland's articles on Elen More. My mum and dad discovered Jackie Crookston in Kenny MacAskill's book on Radical Scotland. My mum also read the manuscript in draft, as did my dear friends Geraldine Bradley and Maolcholm Scott. My thanks to them; all remaining errors are of course mine alone, and I hope that I may beg forgiveness for these particularly from Irish and Welsh readers (and Abigail Burnyeat on the 'Celtic' word).

Biggest thanks of all go to Tom Morgan-Jones, provider of nutrition, pourer of wine and general holder-together of body and soul. You're the best, a ghaoil. Hello!

MAIRI KIDD is a writer, publisher and translator who works by day to support the world of Scottish books and reading as Head of Literature at Creative Scotland. Her previous work includes *Warriors and Witches and Damn Rebel Bitches: Scottish Women to Live Your Life by*. Mairi also writes for children, and has written for stage, screen and radio in Gaelic and English.

Having first been inspired to write about Scotland's women when living in the original home of scandalous society beauty Rachel Chiesley, Lady Grange, Mairi has forsaken seventeenth-century ghosts for a home by the sea in Portobello, where hardy women once hauled the catch to market.